MW00568948

OUR FATHER
The Prodigal Son Returns

PASTOR BRUCE SMITH & PHIL KERSHAW

OUR FATHER

THE PRODIGAL SON RETURNS

FOREWORD BY MICHAEL (PINBALL) CLEMONS

BRUCE SMITH AND PHIL KERSHAW

*This book was made possible by a generous grant from
Mr. Don M. Ross of Jones, Gable & Co. Ltd*

CASTLE QUAY BOOKS

Our Father: The Prodigal Son Returns

Copyright ©2013 Phil Kershaw and Bruce Smith
All rights reserved
Printed in Canada
International Standard Book Number: 978-1-927355-30-5
ISBN 978-1-927355-31-2 EPUB

Published by:
Castle Quay Books
Pickering, Ontario, L1W 1A5
Tel: (416) 573-3249
E-mail: info@castlequaybooks.com   www.castlequaybooks.com

Edited by Ingrid Walter and Lori MacKay
Cover design by Burst Impressions
Printed at Essence Publishing, Belleville, Ontario

Scripture quotations marked NIV are taken from the HOLY BIBLE, NEW INTERNATIONAL VERSION ®. Copyright © 1973, 1978, 1984 by International Bible Society. Used by permission of Zondervan Publishing House. All rights reserved. Scripture quotations marked KJV are from The Holy Bible, King James Version. Copyright © 1977, 1984, Thomas Nelson Inc., Publishers. All rights reserved. Scripture quotations marked NKJV are taken from the New King James Version. Copyright © 1979, 1980, 1982. Thomas Nelson Inc., Publishers. This book or parts thereof may not be reproduced in any form without prior written permission of the publishers.

Library and Archives Canada Cataloguing in Publication

Smith, Bruce, 1949 Mar. 28-
    Our father : the prodigal son returns / foreword by Michael (Pinball) Clemons ; Bruce Smith and Phil Kershaw.
Previous title: Our father, father to the fatherless, c2008.
Also issued in electronic format.

ISBN 978-1-927355-30-5

    1. Smith, Bruce, 1949 Mar. 28-. 2. Fatherless families. 3. Fathers and sons—Religious aspects—Christianity. 4. Congregational churches—Canada—Clergy—Biography. 5. Football players—Canada—Biography. 6. Real estate agents—Canada—Biography. 7. Toronto (Ont.)—Biography. I. Kershaw, Phil, 1948- II. Title.

BX7260.S554A3 2013   285.8092   C2013-901389-X

I dedicate this book to Shirley,
a loving and faithful wife and mother.

"I have fought the good fight, I have finished the race, I have kept the faith." (2 Timothy 4:7, NKJV)

TABLE OF CONTENTS

ACKNOWLEDGEMENTS

I thank God the Father and His son Jesus Christ above all.

This book could not have been written without the support and patience of my loving wife Shirley, who is the best example of Christ I know.

I also thank God for giving us our children, Courtne and Coby. I hope through the writing of this book they will come to understand much about my life as a boy growing up in Texas and how it was very different from theirs.

My mother Dorothy Bradley has been an incredible resource for my some-times-fallible memory, a mother who endured tough times and made many sac-rifices to feed, clothe and educate us as children. Still today, she is the force that keeps our family together although we live thousands of miles apart.

It was "Mamma's Faith" that sustained us and I believe without her prayers I wouldn't be the man I am today.

William Hardy and Peggy Jeanette, who suffered much in silence; my baby sister Donna Latell, who shares the same mother and my half siblings Jessie and Jennie, who share the same father, form an integral part of this book. I embrace them for sharing with me the tears and the laughter.

A great deal of my appreciation goes to Thomas L Caldwell, my first min-istry partner, mentor, friend and "brother," who along with his wife Dorothy have been supportive of my ministry and my efforts to get this story out. As well I must thank Bill and Gayle White for their tremendous encouragement and support of this project.

I thank God for the Sowell family who became like family, especially Dick. Then there are my coaches to thank; the coach who along with his family helped shape and change my destiny, Coach Morris Magee now deceased, his wife Frankie and son Mark, as well as coaches Bob Hopkins, Williams, Johnson, Skeeter, and Black.

OUR FATHER: THE PRODIGAL SON RETURNS

There is no place like Boulder Colorado in the spring and I guess that's why many of my football team mates and friends are still there. Glen Bailey, Lee Richmond, Larry and Sue Brunson, whose lives intertwined with mine, as I battled on the football field and against my demons, thank you for being a part of my life story.

"The Wild Bunch," they too had an impact, Mark "Snakeman," Morris, Chuck "The Black" Holmes, Ron Brinny Dotson, as well as my team mates from the underground gridiron. In addition, there would be no story to write without recollections of those heady days with John Williams and my best friends in the Canadian Football League, George Wells, Eugene Clark, Ron Foxx, Larry "Big Dog" Watkins, Emery Hicks, Larry Brame, and Ron "Swamp Dog" Estay.

Though now deceased, there is no denying Lamar Leachman, Daddy Walter, Uncle Beji, Dwight "Ushay" Smith, Ted Woods, Coach Jerry Williams and Richard Wiseman, all had some influence on my life.

My "Friends for life," Alex and Dory Korn, Margaret Parker, Trevet Thiessen, my sister in law and unofficial family lawyer, I'm glad you are on our team!

Also, thank you to Mr. Wilfred and Mrs. Nora Somers, Shirley's parents for trusting me with your beautiful daughter.

My friends Joe and Mary Santos, Cletus, Angela and Nicole Castelino, friends, prayer partners, vision partners and supporters, you helped motivate me to finish this book, when I might have given up.

Neleitha Hewitt, sister in the Lord, prayer warrior, ministry partner, you have been my rock.

David Rapley, and his wife Joy Rapley, Michael Labanowich and the Rock and River Congregation hold a special place in my heart and soul. Thanks for being there through the journey.

This book might have taken a completely different turn if Pastor Ali had not entered my life and encouraged me to go into ministry. Thanks also to Reverend Dr. Audley James and his wife Pastor Rosenda James, my first spiritual parents.

In addition, I am grateful to King Bay Chaplaincy, especially Pat Kimeda, Reverend Ken Coffield and Jennifer Ismail, for prayers and encouragement, John and Rebecca Hardwood, Purpose at Work partners and our Tuesday morning bible study group. Kris Hansen, Hank Reimer, David Imrie, Robert Cruickshank, Steve Dulmage, David Ekmekjian, Jeff Baldock, Michael Gundy, Paul Noh, Michael Nikiforuk and Charles Waterman.

ACKNOWLEDGEMENTS

Peter and Mary Dallas "Angels on call," your feedback was food for writing this book. Thanks to Bob Cheatley whose enthusiasm after reading the manuscript gave me no option but to finish it.

They say imitation is one of the greatest forms of flattery. Thanks Darin Burns, you are a role model.

Janet Meredith, for her leadership and "stepping up to the plate" and the whole Sparrow way community gave me many reasons to write this book. We hope it will affect the lives of at risk youth in that tiny Toronto enclave and far beyond.

Thanks to Eric Walters who took the time to meet with us and encouraged us when this book was a mere thought, to, "write it!"

To Phil Kershaw my co-author, the thank you list is long. So many great ideas including the title came from Phil, who not only coached me and helped to shape the book's story line, but motivated me to work hard and somehow, to keep pace with him.

My gratitude also goes to Ingrid Walter whose article on fatherthelessness in the *Toronto Star*, "Lost Boys," was one of the main reasons this book was written. I thank her particularly for her candid critiques, the attention she paid to editing each and every chapter and the diligence with which she handled the publishing process.

Bruce Smith
May 2008

FOREWORD BY
MICHAEL "PINBALL" CLEMONS

It is indeed a great privilege and honour to have the opportunity to write the foreword to this extremely important work, *Our Father, the Prodigal Son Returns*. While I'm deeply honoured, I feel profoundly inadequate to pen the prelude to what is the punctuation of the passion and purpose of the life and legacy of Pastor and Pro football All-Star, Bruce "The Bear Man" Smith. This memoir is inspired by his unbridled zeal to mentor and support fatherless boys and appropriately chronicles his own struggles growing up without a stable father figure.

I believe I was chosen because of our uncanny connection, both African Americans raised in southern cities with racial overtones to single parent mothers and both fortuitously parlayed early football success into a platform of access and progress. Ultimately arriving in the CFL where we each won championships, had celebrated careers and retired as Captains of the oldest pro sports franchise in North America, the Toronto Argonauts. However the pages of this book reveal a much more difficult, arduous path for Bruce to this strikingly similar destination. While I was on the heels of the civil rights movement, Bruce rode the crest, replete with its divisive racial tensions and venomous tirades. This coupled with the more hazardous and hurtful absence of his dad paved a tumultuous road to success, lined with an inconsolable sense of loss that often manifested itself into bitterness, anger and hostility.

Bruce's commitment to the issue of fatherlessness is obvious, he's a victim. The statistics that reflect the victim impact of this malignant epidemic are infinitely more staggering, yet our community and greater culture's response to date is virtually benign. More specifically, kids without an engaged father have significantly less education, a higher risk of suicide and a greater propensity for violent behavior, addiction to drugs, jail time and teenage pregnancy. That's why the big

13

man with the undeniable presence and the booming baritone decided to commit his voice to this oft referenced and more often neglected malady.

It probably wouldn't surprise you if I told you our life stories continued to effortlessly intertwine. We both made Toronto our domicile of choice and capably navigated the more tenuous transition of life after football, Bruce becoming one of the most successful real estate agents in the country. But our greatest kinship is unquestionably our devout faith, love for family and commitment to kids and community. We lived parallel lives that surprisingly rarely intersected. We often talked about working together more closely and I believe we both thought one day we would. Unfortunately, Bruce passed, for most of us too soon. However, Bruce and I have finally come to that crossroad, with this commentary I officially join Bruce "The Bear Man" Smith in his effort to support, mentor, love and inspire the fatherless.

By the way, even after his athletic and entrepreneurial success Bruce still struggled...but finally found the answer. My job was to get you to look for it!

Rest in peace Bruce and thanks for all you did for others, especially the fatherless. My thoughts and prayers are with your beautiful wife Shirley, your children Courtne and Coby and your family back in Texas. It is my sincere hope that we can keep your work and ministry alive on behalf of fatherless kids everywhere.

INTRODUCTION

Sadly, Bruce Smith's earthly journey ended on January 3, 2013, when the prodigal son from Gainesville, Texas, by way of Huntsville, Texas, Boulder, Colorado, and Toronto, Ontario, Canada, returned to his Heavenly Father.

I am sure that there was a great welcome there and that God gave him the ultimate accolade for a life well-lived in service to the Lord and said, "*Well done, good and faithful servant*" (Matthew 25:21 NKJV).

I met Bruce in 2004 through a mutual friend, Darin Burns. Darin, who ran a number of fitness businesses I had worked with as a consultant, had a long history with Bruce. It started when as a young boy he was put into a group home by an abusive father. He was befriended by Smith, who was at that time a star defensive lineman for the Canadian Football League's Toronto Argonauts.

This was daunting stuff for a troubled kid with a dubious future, but it inspired Burns to turn his life around. He went on to play football in the CFL as well and forged a successful business career.

I had a long history in the CFL as an executive with the Saskatchewan and Ottawa Rough Riders and CFL chairman in the 1990s, so Bruce and I had a common history and hit it off immediately.

I quickly recognized that, as well as being a literal "larger than life" figure, Bruce could be a pivotal figure in changing people's lives for good. This also was coincidental to my own spiritual reawakening, and it all came together in early 2005 when we both attended a business meeting in Toronto. When he came over to me I heard a voice, which I now believe was God's, say three words: "Help this man."

This led to an amazing odyssey of spiritual growth and increasing faith for me, and Bruce Smith was the catalyst that made it happen.

OUR FATHER: THE PRODIGAL SON RETURNS

It manifested itself several months later during the notorious "Summer of the Gun" in Toronto of 2005 in which there were 52 gun murders in Toronto, of primarily black young men. I remember clearly sitting in a Tim Hortons restaurant in Mississauga (it doesn't get any more Canadian than that) and reading the "Summer of the Gun" headline in the *Toronto Sun*. I called Bruce to say that with his background of being raised in segregated Texas and now as a major figure in Toronto—he was a chaplain at King-Bay Chaplaincy and had his own ministry—he could help.

Bruce thought about it and got back to me. He believed that the guns, drugs and gangs were a symptom of the root problem, which was fatherlessness. He went on to say he knew this was true because of his own experience of having his biological father abandon him and his siblings when he was a small child. It had taken him the better part of a lifetime to process and overcome it.

This led to a decision to write this book about the whole issue of fatherlessness, initially published in 2008. Through the kind auspices of Larry Willard of Castle-Quay Books we are able to present this updated and revised version to bring this very important issue to a much wider audience.

If you think that the evidence of the scourge of fatherlessness is primarily anecdotal, then consider the following:

- 90% of homeless and runaway children are from fatherless homes [US D.H.H.S., Bureau of the Census]
- 80% of rapists motivated with displaced anger come from fatherless homes. [*Criminal Justice & Behavior*, Vol 14, pp. 403–26, 1978]
- 71% of pregnant teenagers lack a father. [U.S. Department of Health and Human Services press release, Friday, March 26, 1999]
- 63% of youth suicides are from fatherless homes. [US D.H.H.S., Bureau of the Census]
- 85% of children who exhibit behavioral disorders come from fatherless homes. [Center for Disease Control]
- 90% of adolescent repeat arsonists live with only their mother. [Wray Herbert, "Dousing the Kindlers," *Psychology Today*, January, 1985, p. 28]
- 71% of high school dropouts come from fatherless homes. [National Principals Association Report on the State of High Schools]
- 75% of adolescent patients in chemical abuse centers come from fatherless homes. [Rainbows for all God's Children]

INTRODUCTION

- 70% of juveniles in state operated institutions have no father. [US Department of Justice, Special Report, Sept. 1988]
- 85% of youths in prisons grew up in a fatherless home. [Fulton County Georgia jail populations, Texas Department of Corrections, 1992]
- Fatherless boys and girls are: twice as likely to drop out of high school; twice as likely to end up in jail; four times more likely to need help for emotional or behavioral problems. [US D.H.H.S. news release, March 26, 1999]

(Source: "Statistics," The Fatherless Generation, http://thefatherlessgeneration. wordpress.com/statistics/. Most of the research on this topic is U.S. based, but the findings can be projected universally.)

This problem is compounded when you consider that in the African-American community, for instance, the percentage of children born to unwed mothers is now in the range of 75 percent.

It is clear that the destruction of the traditional nuclear family and changed attitudes towards sex and procreation are having a devastating impact. We are now and will continue to face a bitter harvest of violent, dangerous young men without the skills and tools to make proper life decisions, and all of us will pay the price.

This important book is Bruce's memoir of how being fatherless impacted his own life. It allows us to better understand that a lonely, heartbroken child looking for a loving father will likely morph into a confused, angry young man who will take out his rage and hostility on the world at large.

The good news is that through the saving grace of Jesus Christ Bruce turned his life around, and these young men can too, because God is the *"father of the fatherless"* (Psalm 68:5 NKJV).

I also want the world to know that Bruce Smith was not just a former football player turned pastor who was a crusader on the fatherlessness issue. He was a huge giant of the faith and impacted the lives of countless people.

Pat Kimeda, who worked with Bruce at King-Bay Chaplaincy, said Bruce talked and prayed numerous people who wandered into their offices at their wits' end out of taking their lives. That's to say nothing of the people he visited in jail, hospital and their homes to minister to them and change their destinies forever.

My deep gratitude goes out to the people who have made this book possible: Larry Willard, Castle Quay Publishing, Don Ross, Tom Caldwell, Ingrid Walter (who helped edit and acted as publisher of the original version),

Pat Kimeda, Darin Burns, Bill White, Jeff Baldock and others; without their very valuable contribution this couldn't have happened. Thank you as well to Michael "Pinball" Clemons for his eloquent foreword, and Lorna Dueck, Tom Shepherd, Senator David Tkachuk, Leo Ezerins, and Chima Obidigbo for their heartfelt endorsements.

I also owe a personal debt of gratitude to supporters of this project like Angela and Cletus Castelino, Linda Bradshaw, Janet Meredith and Neleitha Hewitt, who supported Bruce and this project for many years.

Finally I want to thank Bruce for his priceless friendship and inspirational leadership. He changed my life for the good, helping me back to God and Christ so I could pursue the path that the Lord had chosen for me. I thank God as well for Bruce's amazing, magnificent family—his wife, Shirley, his children, Courtne and Coby, and his Texas family, in particular his sister Peggy Maxey, who has been so supportive. I pray that the Lord will continue to be with them and bless them forever.

Bruce's earthly work is done, but the cause of raising and mentoring father-less boys goes on. It is my fervent hope that his amazing life will inspire a new generation of Kingdom warriors, who will pick up the mantle and continue this divine assignment.

Just as the apostle Paul's writings in the years following Jesus' resurrection became the foundation of the Christian faith that we practice two thousand years after His passing, so in some small measure may Bruce's words continue to live on to inspire the fatherless to connect with their Heavenly Father.

God bless,
Phil Kershaw

ONE

THE SKUNK CREEK INN

These men lie in wait for their own blood; they waylay only themselves! (Proverbs 1:18 NIV).

What seemed like a scene from one of our favourite movies, Sam Peckinpah's western classic *The Wild Bunch*, was about to become a reality. However, there were no stunt men, only a bunch of black youths pretending to be hit men. We were not men in black but young black men caught up in a web of gangs, guns, drugs, sex and violence that would change the course of our lives forever.

I armed myself with a .38 automatic fully loaded pistol with an extra clip, while my 12-gauge lay on the ground beside me. Snakeman had his finger on the trigger of his sawed-off shotgun. Chuck, who liked hand-to-hand combat, outfitted himself with a pair of brass knuckles and a lead pipe wrapped with black tape. Dotson was partial to knives, so he carried a large one.

Snakeman positioned himself at the side of the building facing the front door of Skunk Creek Inn, while I knelt towards the rear of my car. "Black Goat," as everyone called her, was the best camouflage in the dark night. Chuck and Dotson crouched at the side of the building facing the inn. There was no way out now; we were in too deep. What started out as a typical Friday night of hanging out, hustling girls and money for a midnight snack, was about to turn nasty.

It was a hot summer night, and as usual we had decided we would work up a little sweat indoors. Skunk Creek had a reputation for the best live music and attracting Colorado's finest women. We roared up to the club in Black Goat. As usual, I parked her a few meters from the front door, a no-parking zone, but I always got away with it.

OUR FATHER: THE PRODIGAL SON RETURNS

By this time, the place was packed with a long line of students and locals waiting to get in. All eyes trailed us as we walked past the party hopefuls with our duster coats hovering around our knees and our fingers protruding from our sawed-off woollen gloves. The night's bouncers greeted us with the usual arrogant nod.

Snakeman, Chuck, Dotson and I made our way to our usual spots where we could check out the scene and look at the night's eye candy. My position was always on the landing, where I could see the action around the bar and the dance floor. While Chuck and Dotson got a close-up view mingling through the crowd, Snakeman was milling around looking for his next victim, usually an unsuspecting white student just out to have some fun.

It was especially packed that night. A popular band from Denver was performing with two guys whose talent was so large they would end up playing with the mighty Earth, Wind and Fire. Their presence attracted a larger than normal crowd. Unknown to us, some soul brothers from Denver had entered the club looking to muscle in on the night's crop of girls, even though it was clear that many were spoken for. They were easy to spot because we knew all the regular black guys who hung out at Skunk Creek Inn.

Snakeman's school brother from Denver told him about what they had planned for us, so we made sure we always knew where they were and what they were doing. Another brother told us they were packing guns. What nerve, we thought. This was our backyard.

Snakeman decided to play a little head game with one of the Denver boys to see whether they really had the guts to try to muscle in on our territory. We had decided it was time to teach these rookies a lesson. We walked outside and waited.

It seemed like an eternity.

Finally, they began to stroll out. As we were about to pounce, someone in the crowd yelled, "That guy has a gun! Somebody call the cops."

As we scrambled to get out of there, Snakeman convinced two girls to come with us. We jumped into our car with the girls sitting in the back seat and Snakeman riding shotgun.

After driving around for a while we pulled into a 7–11. A couple of minutes later, a cop car pulled up next to us. Our hearts were beating like conga drums, but we carried on as if everything was fine. To my surprise, they asked if we were with the Buffaloes.

Playing college football in Colorado definitely had its privileges. As we mouthed a loud "Yes," one of the cops leaned over and peeked into the back seat. "You boys stay out of trouble now," he said. Had those cops seen our guns, I probably wouldn't be here today to tell this story. Those cops never saw those guns because they lay quietly underneath the girls in the back seat.

That night I had a sense we had experienced some kind of divine intervention.

Listen to evil voices
They will lead you
To wrong choices.

TWO

IN THE BEGINNING

He will turn the heart of the fathers to the children, and the hearts of the children to the fathers (Malachi 4:6 NIV).

My biological father abandoned our family and left for California before I was two years old, leaving Mamma with me, my three brothers and sisters to raise by herself.

The *New Oxford Dictionary* defines a father as "a man who gives care and protection." The word *parent* is from the Greek word meaning "to protect." When I think of the word *protect* I think of making someone feel safe and secure, which is one of the main responsibilities of parents, especially fathers. I don't ever remember feeling secure as a child. I could never understand why we had no father.

I wasn't fatherless at birth; however, my father neglected me even while Mamma was pregnant. He had abandoned her emotionally, causing me to feel her pain and shame.

I was born on March 28, 1949, in Gainesville, Texas. According to my birth certificate, my father was William Hardy Smith, age 26, and my mother's was Dorothy Lee Smith, age 21. The birth certificates list them as Negroes.

It showed my father's occupation as "labourer" and my mother's as "house-wife" and that my father served in the U.S. army and received an honourable discharge. The certificate says William and Dorothy were the parents of two other children, my oldest brother, William Hardy Smith Jr., and my older sister, Peggy Jeanette Smith. Although my birth certificate listed my father's name, he was a father in name only.

I never really knew why our father abandoned us, but many black fathers left the south and went to places like Chicago, Detroit and California to find work. However more often than not, they would also find other women, which led to starting new families and leaving the other family behind, as in our case. Now as an adult and having studied the situation it is not so mysterious. The simple fact is that a black man was hard pressed to make a decent living at the time in the segregated south. This was compounded after World War II when men like my father who had put their lives on the line to fight for their country, came home only to realize that they couldn't even sit at a lunch counter or use the same washroom as their white counterparts, so they upped and left for greener pastures, and sadly the destruction of the black family was a negative by-product of this.

Apart from my state of fatherlessness, there were many other things I didn't understand as a child growing up in the fifties and sixties in small-town Texas. I knew at a very young age that white people considered us inferior. We couldn't eat with them, live with them, go to the same school as them. We couldn't drink from the same water fountain. In fact, we couldn't even order our ice cream from the same parlour window.

Even though I didn't understand why things were that way, I understood that being black and living in Texas meant you were second class and second rate. It meant you were not as good as a white kid. At the time, I accepted that as the truth. It was just another hope breaker. Most white kids had fathers, but many of us black kids didn't, and in the fifties, even though more black fathers stuck around than today, absentee fathers seemed to be the norm rather than the exception.

Mamma finished high school, but like many of the black moms who were single, she worked as a maid for a white family. Most of her friends had jobs as servants for white families or as maids in motels. Mamma worked for a white family that owned a clothing store in town called California's. It wasn't a place where black people could afford to shop, but I know these people really seemed to like Mamma. I remember them being happy for her when she got married but sad when she had to quit when we moved to Huntsville.

They had two boys a little older than William and me. They would often give Mamma their slightly worn clothes. To us this was like getting brand new stuff. They fit William perfectly, but unfortunately for me the clothes were too small and the shoes too tight. Mamma cooked and cleaned, and she would often bring home leftovers, which we looked forward to getting. The first thing our eyes would search for as she walked through the door was something wrapped in tinfoil.

I really don't know how Mamma did it, but in many ways it seemed we were better off with her as the sole provider than we were after she remarried.

IN THE BEGINNING

Gainesville was and still is a small town, and even at an early age I couldn't wait until I was old enough to move to a big city like Dallas or Fort Worth. Another thing about living in a small town like Gainesville was that we could walk or ride our bikes from one side of town to another to visit friends.

We often took shortcuts through white neighbourhoods. However, many times angry whites chased us, hurling both racial insults and, sometimes, rocks. A group of older guys would go through these white neighbourhoods on purpose, enticing the white kids to chase us back into our territory, where a gang of black kids would be hiding out, ready to retaliate with rocks and bottles.

Once some angry white kids chased me, and I hurried over a brick wall to escape. As I ran I could hear gunshots in the distance. At the time blacks weren't allowed to be buried in the same cemetery as whites. How ironic that I would be coached as a professional football player in 1979 by former Green Bay Packer great, Hall of Famer and living legend Forrest Gregg, whose wife's parents are now buried in the same cemetery as my grandmother.

My best friend in Gainesville was Roger Sherman, who lived next door. He had a bunch of sisters and several brothers. His mamma's name was Tootsie. Mamma and Tootsie had once been good friends. I don't know what went wrong between them, but I know Tootsie had a son by a man Mamma dated.

At that time, we were living in an upstairs flat owned by Miss Simpson. We used to hang out a lot at Roger's because he lived in a house with a big yard. I had a huge crush on one of his sisters.

I remember the first time we moved into a house. Even though it was rented it was nice having our own yard because it meant I didn't have to go over to someone else's house, which gave me more time to play outside.

There were some advantages living in small towns like Gainesville and Huntsville. Everyone knew you and who your Mamma was. It was like having extra eyes watching you. A lot of times I heard, "I'm going to tell your mamma on you, boy." There was much more of a sense of community because we knew all of our neighbours, and everyone sort of looked after each other.

In the fifties and sixties, both Gainesville and Huntsville were segregated, but I remember playing with some white kids, folks in our neighbourhood everybody called white trash.

Butch was one white kid who was hard to forget. It wasn't only because he played with us; he also had an unusual handicap. He had no legs and used his arms as his legs to get around.

While we were outcasts because of the colour of our skin, Butch was an outcast because of his handicap. Even though he was considered white trash by some of his white peers, being white still meant he had many privileges we didn't have. While it was okay to play together outside, there was no way we were allowed into his house.

It was easy to figure out where the coloured folks lived in Gainesville and Huntsville. It was where most of the houses were dilapidated and you could find lots of kids playing on the streets, many dirty with snotty noses and hair that hadn't been combed.

The one thing I can say about Mamma, she always kept a clean house, even though it was only a step above a shack. Every weekend she would make us help her clean up the house. Some of us would sweep while the others dusted. We also had to clean up our rooms, make our beds and take turns doing the dishes. She taught us how to iron, which I still do today.

Mamma liked nice things and really liked to decorate, so she kept the house looking good, especially the living room. Even though we didn't have a lot of clothes, we were always clean, and our hair was combed. When we were little she used to wash us in a tin tub using the stove to warm up the water.

To be honest, it seemed we got along better than some of the kids who had a daddy. But insecurity and hurt over not having a dad followed me everywhere, and so I built up all kinds of defences to protect myself, like pretending to be tough and not to really care that I had no father.

Where I grew up, there were lots of mothers and grandmothers. They acted as the matriarchs. It wasn't that lots of men weren't around. There were just very few fathers who represented any definition you would find in a dictionary.

More often than not, the one providing the care and protection in a family was the mother or the grandmother, and in many cases the provision too. It was not unusual to see children in the same home who had the same mother but different biological fathers.

Mamma did her best to be both mother and father to us kids. Mamma wasn't mean or anything like that; she just made sure we knew who was boss. One thing I know for sure—we didn't talk back to Mamma or swear or use God's name in vain, because Mamma made it real clear she would knock us out, and when she talked like that, we knew she was serious.

She wouldn't hesitate to put her foot down, as well as our pants, when necessary to teach us respect. I laugh when I think of some of the whippings I got from Mamma. According to her, most of my whippings were because I always had to have the last word. I remember one time I decided I would run to avoid the switch. She chased me around the neighbourhood for several hours until I wore her out. Then she got my sister Peggy and my older brother William involved in the chase until I wore them out too. I finally stopped running, but before going home I sought sanctuary from Miss Simpson, the lady who rented Mamma the one-bedroom flat over her garage.

She was like a second grandmother. She would often babysit us until Mamma came home from work or when she went out dancing with her friends. Rumour had it that Mamma was quite a dancer. I didn't like it when Mamma left us there overnight, because Miss Simpson made us go to bed early, usually on a pallet on the floor. I always had a hard time sleeping because she had this big ole wind-up floor clock. I would just lie there counting every tick, and on every hour there was this big gong.

She also had a swing on her front porch. When I was about six, I was swinging with a girl named Debra Manuel. When we got off the swing, I asked her to play an adult version of show-and-tell. We were just about to start when I heard Miss Simpson's feet on the dusty road coming toward us. In my haste to cover up what I had done, I got a very sensitive part of my anatomy caught in my zipper. Miss Simpson freed me, but the bad news was that she told Mamma.

That evening it took a long time before I eventually got the nerve to head home. Mamma went on as though nothing had happened. She made dinner as usual and finally got us three boys and one girl in the same bed. I fell fast asleep. Then all of a sudden I felt this sting across my behind. There was Mamma with her big leather belt, administering perfectly aimed and timed licks to my butt. All I can say is, when she finished with me, my X-rated show-and-tell with Debra Manuel was over.

At eight years old I decided to run away from home. After packing a few things in a bag, I figured I would head for Tulsa to live with my Aunt Sally. I had spent a summer with her and her husband, Uncle Timothy, in Tulsa when I was five. Rumour was they wanted to adopt me because they had no children at the time.

My plan was to hitchhike and maybe hop a train like a hobo. I hadn't gone too far before William and Peggy caught up to me, riding their bikes. Mamma was waiting at the front door, and after she gave me her special medicine, I never tried that again.

There is no way I could stay out past midnight. Mamma would come looking for me. I couldn't come home wearing some fancy new shoes or gear either.

I can't say I had the fear of the Lord at that age, but I sure had a healthy fear of Mamma, and so did the rest of us.

I remember one time some of my friends and I went into town. This was one of the highlights as a kid because we could look at all the stuff and day-dream that maybe Santa would bring us some of these nice gifts on Christmas if we were good.

Saturday was a big day in Gainesville, and everybody headed for the five and dime or Kresge's downtown to buy something special. I can't recall why, but we let Dwight tag along with us that day. I also remember that spinning tops were the "in" things at the time. As usual we didn't have any money, and we didn't want to wait for Christmas to get our tops. We went around to several stores until we found one where there was only one person working.

There were at least five of us plus Dwight, so a couple of the kids distracted the lady who was working there while the rest of us helped ourselves to some tops. When Dwight saw this he started to cry, "I'm gonna tell Mamma!" He wouldn't shut up, so we got nervous and quickly hurried out of the store with the tops.

I figured if the woman saw us we might go to jail, and if not Dwight was going to rat me out, and Mamma, who was my Supreme Ruler at the time, would administer her own justice, which would be the strap, plus probably house arrest.

I was scared to go back and more afraid to go home. I decided to return the hot tops.

The lady in the store was shocked, first that we would steal from the store and then that we would return the stuff. It was also one of the first times I had a real "crisis of conscience." Let's face it, it was the wrath of Mamma that made my blood run cold, but also a voice in my head said, "This is wrong, and because it's wrong, the consequences are not going to be pleasant."

I did the right thing, which was to go back and "repent" to the lady in the store and make it right, and because I did the right thing I avoided disaster. I had to do this in spite of the peer pressure of the group; not everybody who stole a top took it back.

We would usually get home from school before Mamma got in from work. Even though she wasn't there, she had a sixth sense. Once we sneaked off and went swimming in the gravel pit. Mamma was always warning us about going swimming. It seemed like every year someone we knew drowned in some unauthorized swimming hole.

IN THE BEGINNING

I always wanted to be accepted, so I went swimming with the older kids even though I knew Mamma would be mad if she found out. I thought I had gotten away with it, but my eyes betrayed me. They were very red, and it wasn't long after she got home from work when she began her interrogation. I swore up and down I hadn't been swimming, and she just kept saying, "Boy, don't you lie to me; it's going to be a lot worse if you're lying to me!"

She herded me into the bathroom and pulled out of the hamper my wet underwear with red clay from the gravel pit. Man, she wore me out, and believe me, I never did that again.

Despite the licks, we knew Mamma loved us. She was always there to comfort us or to patch us up after a scrape or a fall, like the time William and I were on our way home after playing at friends. I forgot something and had to go back. No sooner had I stepped into the yard than their big dog attacked me and ripped open my upper lip.

I ran all the way home crying, and by the time I got there, I was covered in blood. She rushed me to the hospital for a rabies shot and stitches. Even though I was only around six it took five nurses and Mamma to hold me down. I still remember the doctor saying, "He's going to be very big and strong by the time he gets to twelve."

Another time I was trying to pry open a can with my hand to get at the last sardine, and my hand slipped and ripped wide open. It was back to the doctor, for another shot and more stitches.

One morning I was outside playing with William, and he told me to pick up a bumblebee. Like a fool, I did, and of course it stung me. I ran in the house crying like a siren, and as usual, Mamma was there to comfort me.

One of my best memories is the Christmas I got my first bike. After tossing, turning and getting up several times to check if Santa ate the cookies and drank the milk we left for him, I finally fell asleep, only to be awakened by a big thud. I found out later that what I thought was Santa Claus was actually Mamma and her best friend, Margaret, falling down while trying to get my new bike up the stairs in the dark. I think Mamma and her friend had a little too much Christmas cheer. I woke up Christmas morning, and the first thing I saw was my brand new red bike. The next day Mamma pushed me and held me up until I learned to ride.

Thank God for mothers who care enough to stay with their kids and teach them respect, even with the aid of a strap or my Mamma's instrument of choice, a strong switch. I will forever be grateful for the mother God chose for me.

OUR FATHER: THE PRODIGAL SON RETURNS

I know there are many
Who don't agree with Mamma's ways
But I am convinced
They helped to keep me from an early grave.

THREE

SINS OF THE FATHER

"For I, the LORD your God, am a jealous God, visiting the iniquity of the fathers upon the children to the third and fourth generations of those who hate Me, but showing mercy to thousands, to those who love Me and keep My commandments"
(Exodus 20:5-6, NKJV).

I looked a lot like my daddy, Mamma said. He was a big man well over six feet, large and loud, two traits I definitely inherited from him. He also had a good sense of humour.

The first time I remember seeing my real father I was 11. He came to Gainesville to take us to spend the summer with him in California.

I remember him driving up in this big shiny black Cadillac. I was so excited I was jumping up and down, until I saw this cute little black Barbie-doll looking woman sitting where my mamma should have been. Immediately I decided I would never like her and that I would make her life hell on earth.

My first plan was to stage a hunger strike, not realizing this would be a three-day drive to California. I remember making our first pit stop for food after leaving Gainesville at around 8 p.m. I tried to talk Dwight, my baby brother, into joining me, but he wimped out.

There I was, sitting in the back seat by myself while they were all in the restaurant. They seemed to take forever. When they finally came out, my brothers and sister were carrying on with this woman like she was our mamma. I pretended to be sleep until she said, "Bruce, I bought you a burger with french fries."

"I don't want it!" I growled. She smiled and politely placed it where I could smell it. I waited for several hours until I thought everyone except Dad, who was

31

driving, was asleep, then quietly picked up the brown paper bag to sneak a few fries. Of course they all heard me and burst out laughing.

I would end up having the last laugh, because after we got to California my father and the black Barbie kept getting into fights, and apparently they had something to do with me. One time he packed up her stuff and threw it out on the porch. She left that evening and went to stay somewhere else. I'm sure their fights had to do with a lot more than just me, but I felt good thinking I might have contributed to her leaving.

We had a lot of fun that summer. We went to the beach and several times to a popular theme park nearby. I also attended my very first professional football game. The Dallas Cowboys were in town to play against the Los Angeles Rams at the LA Coliseum.

I'll never forget that night, because we got on the wrong bus going home after the game and ended up miles and miles away from home. To make matters worse, the buses stopped running and we had to walk. Man, we walked for hours, with William leading the way, before we finally made it home.

While in California, I discovered that my father had several women on the side. He was proud to introduce us to them, even letting me listen to him talking to one of them on the phone about what they were going to do when they got together, if you know what I mean. I decided right then I wanted to be just like him. I later found myself saying some of the same things I heard him say to his girlfriend to the girls I knew back home.

Mamma also had a lot of relatives living in California, and from time to time we visited one of them named Aunt Dollie. Like her sister Aunt Dorothy, she was an amazing cook and an even better baker. She had a daughter we called Punkin, and she lived on the third floor with her husband.

I also discovered pornography on that trip when I found a *Playboy* magazine under the bed on the third floor in Aunt Dollie's house. I was determined that when I grew up I would have a few bunnies of my own.

In many ways meeting my real father was the beginning of my journey to manhood, but it was also the loss of my innocence. This description of my father unfortunately still holds true for many fathers today who believe having lots of women makes them real men. I had contact with my earthly father, and I got to spend some time with him that holiday, but we never really connected.

My biological father was not exactly the great man I had imagined and certainly not the kind of role model God would have had in mind. He was my real father all right, but he was not equipped or prepared to accept the responsibility of being a father to his children. I had to deal with the painful realization that he was with a woman who was not my mother, raising kids that weren't his. I was 11 years old, confused and hurt. We all called him Smitty, which is what the black Barbie and her two girls called him.

My father turned out to be what you might call a guest father. He was not the constant figure of protection, provision and security a child looks for and needs.

He didn't stay in touch with me after our visit in California, and it would be almost ten years before I saw or heard from him again. Over time, this bred resentment and scorn for him, the other woman and her kids.

In 1969, my sophomore year at the University of Colorado, I decided to go to California for spring break and while there to try to see him. Twelve years had passed since I last saw him. I was now twenty.

It was the sixties, and Afros and bell-bottoms were fashionable. I showed up at his house unannounced, sporting a huge Afro and wearing bell-bottoms, a headband and a vest without a shirt, to expose my long, buff arms.

I remember ringing the doorbell and hearing a loud voice on the other side of the door saying, "It's some damned hippie kid!"

I yelled, "No it isn't. It's Bruce, your damned son!"

He welcomed me in and really seemed happy to see me. He was still with the black Barbie, who turned out to be nice. I was surprised to see a picture of me in my football uniform as a freshman proudly displayed on the coffee table. Apparently someone he worked with had seen me playing on national TV, and he had called Mamma and asked her to send him a picture of me. I guess he wanted to know what I looked like just in case I made it big as a pro, so he could come and get his cut. I know that sounds cruel, but absentee fathers do that to successful kids more often than you may think. They have this sense of entitlement even though they had no shame in abandoning their kids and shirking their responsibility as fathers and providers.

He let my friends and I stay there and drive his new Cadillac, and he made dinner for us. One of my college friends who lived in California came to the house to take us out.

While we were there, my friends and I ran out of money. My father let me use the phone to call Mamma in Texas to tell her where I was and that all was well. While I was talking to Mamma, I asked her to have my stepfather send me some money. I guess my real father overheard part of the conversation. After I hung up, he asked me if I needed money.

OUR FATHER: THE PRODIGAL SON RETURNS

I will never forget the look on his face when I told him everything was fine, that Daddy—referring to Ernest—was sending me money. I could tell he was a little embarrassed and even a little hurt, and I must admit I was glad. Maybe now he realized how much he had hurt me. I had learned to survive without him, and my stepfather, Ernest, had now superseded my birth father as provider and protector.

To my knowledge, he never sent Mamma any money to help support us, so the idea of asking him for help never crossed my mind. Looking back, I was being cruel, but I wanted my father to understand how much of a deadbeat dad he was. He had abandoned the family when I was a small child and left us to fend for ourselves while he started a new life with another woman and her children, far away, seemingly not caring or feeling any remorse for deserting his own children.

What I didn't understand then but appreciate now is that both my father and I were sons and grandsons whose negative behaviour was influenced by iniquity. We were both victims of secret faults that we had inherited from our forefathers and were caught in the cycle of generational sin.

Fathers don't force your new Barbie on your kids
Or they will resent you and her
Just like I did.

FOUR

MAMMA'S FAITH

I call to remembrance the genuine faith that is in you, which first
dwelt in your grandmother (2 Timothy 1:5 NKJV).

Texas is part of the Bible belt, so it was taken for granted that everyone believed in God. Talking about God or prayer was part of life in the South. Even the KKK claimed to be carrying out their own despicable brand of terrorism in the name of the Lord.

Mamma, like most other black mothers and grandmothers, had faith in God. Even though going to church was usually reserved for Sundays, praying was a daily routine. The only "white" person allowed in our house, Mamma used to say, was the Lord, and I guess that was because you couldn't see Him.

I don't remember a time when Mamma didn't pray and acknowledge God by giving thanks. We always said grace before we ate, whether at home or at someone else's house.

We would usually take turns saying grace. Mamma also prayed with us before bed and taught us bedtime prayers. Even when I stopped going to church after leaving for university I still said my prayers before going to bed.

Another thing I remember is Mamma dragging us to church on Sundays and sometimes even twice. She would dress us in our Sunday best, which included a suit, shirt and tie most of the time.

Naturally we went to an all-black church; we were Baptists. Uncle Beji played the piano and sang solos, and my grandmother, Junior, sang in the choir. There were a lot more mothers in church than fathers. Very seldom would you find a black family that didn't believe in the Lord and that didn't go to church, and even if they didn't, most people in our neighbourhood still believed in Him and had respect for God. There was fear of God even when people didn't follow

Him or His commandments. I was always puzzled when people who didn't go to church called on Him when they were in a jam or in trouble, never thinking that one day I would be one of them.

Church was not an option in our household; we went whether we wanted to or not. Even though it was more religion than relationship with God, I know looking back that valuable seeds of faith were sown, the fruit of which would change my life many years later. It would be Mamma's faith in God that would sustain her as she fought to keep the family together.

It was her faith that would sustain her when she would one day battle cancer and win. It would be Mamma's faith that would keep her from falling apart when those closest to her hurt her heart, including me. Her faith in God would sustain her when she found out my stepfather was having an affair with a younger woman even while she battled cancer. It would be her faith in God's faithfulness that would one day turn her sorrow into joy.

However, as a kid going to church, to me it just seemed like a waste of time. I would rather be playing football or something. Even in the service, I would always be daydreaming or squirming in my seat, wishing I was somewhere else. Many times Mamma would either kick my foot or give me that look that said, "Boy, when I'm finished with you, you won't be able to sit down for days!" which was one of her regular warnings.

At eight years old I was baptized in the baptismal pool in the basement of the church. I had to change clothes after being dunked like a doughnut, but that was about all that changed. I was still a bully and mad at the world.

God to me was no different than having an earthly father. I believed in God just like I believed I had an earthly father. My earthly father had rejected and abandoned me, so I felt God had abandoned and rejected me too.

After all, if there was a God, why would He allow me to be born black with nappy hair and big lips? Why would He allow my father to abandon us? Why would He give me a stepfather who would beat me like a dog? Moreover, why would He allow white people to look down on us like we were nothing but animals?

In fact, white people treated their animals with more dignity than they treated us. It was easy for me to believe that God was more partial to white folk than to us. In my mind, we would have even been the last in line behind the animals and at the back of the boat on Noah's ark.

Trust me, I asked God these kinds of questions, but He was silent on the matter.

MAMMA'S FAITH

There were times when I would get so angry with Mamma that I would say things like "I wish I didn't have a mamma," or worse, that I wished she would die. Then I would beg Him for forgiveness and plead with Him not to take Mamma to heaven yet. I was horrified at the thought of seeing Mamma lying dead in a casket like my grandfather. I had a fear of being abandoned again.

Mothers…
God feels your pain
And sees your tears,
So, don't stop praying
And He'll remove your fears.

FIVE

SEEDS OF FATHERLESSNESS

"By their fruit you will recognize them. Do people pick grapes from thornbushes, or figs from thistles? Likewise every good tree bears good fruit, but a bad tree bears bad fruit"
(Matthew 7:16-17 NIV).

"Behold, a sower went out to sow" (Matthew 13:3 NKJV).

My father and many other men like him remind me of a popular song by the legendary group the Temptations: "Papa was a rolling stone. Wherever he laid his hat was his home." I don't know how many places he laid his hat, but he was real busy planting seeds, and not the kind of righteous sowing the Lord intended when He said, "Be fruitful and go forth and multiply." Only God knows how many siblings I have between the army, Gainesville and California.

My family tree reminds me more of a fruit tree with different kinds of fruit. Besides William and Peggy, who were my whole brother and sister, there were two older half-sisters, Jessie Mary and Jenny, from our father's first marriage, plus a big surprise, another half-sister, born around the same time as me in the same hospital. To this day I have never met her. Then there was a half-brother, Dwight, as well as another half-sister, Donna, whose father was Mamma's second husband, Ernest.

I was back in Gainesville recently, and my older brother, William, informed me that there is one more to add to my father's family tree. Apparently we have another half-brother who was born in California, but not from our father's common-law wife. Little did she know how much she had in common with Mamma and countless other women. They all had the same man, and I had other siblings, some unknown to me, from the seeds of the same father with different mothers.

OUR FATHER: THE PRODIGAL SON RETURNS

There were several men in our life when we were growing up in Gainesville. I can't say I ever thought of any of them as a replacement for a real father.

The closest thing to a father for me as a kid was my step-grandfather, whom we called Daddy Walter. His grandmother was a native Indian and his grandfather a white man from Sweden. Daddy Walter's mother was mixed, and his father was black. This kind of race mixing just wasn't supposed to happen in the southern U.S., but it did, and often. Daddy Walter was my grandmother's second husband.

I never knew my grandfather on my mother's side. The one and only time I saw him, he was in a casket at his funeral. The memory of him lying dead in that casket haunted me for years. Mamma described him as a player, a ladies' man.

I did spend some time with my grandfather on my father's side. His name was Rufus. He lived in Denton, Texas, about a half-hour drive from Gainesville. He would pick us up from time to time to spend weekends with him and his second wife, Pauline. Mamma described Rufus as a player too. When I was young, she said I reminded her of both of my grandfathers, and she didn't mean looks only.

You would think someone called Daddy Walter would be like a big old cuddly teddy bear. Daddy Walter was more like a big mean old grizzly bear. Without a doubt, he was the biggest, scariest man I had ever seen. To me he seemed over nine feet tall, and his hands were so big that it seemed he could hold us kids in the palm of one hand. His size, sinister looks and reputation made me very uncomfortable around him.

I could also sense some tension between Mamma and Daddy Walter. I believe part of it was because of Daddy Walter's treatment of Junior, Mamma's mother. Junior had several nervous breakdowns, and I think Mamma felt Daddy Walter had something to do with it.

There was also talk of Daddy Walter having other women on the side, which was a common thing when I was growing up. I remember we used to drive over with Daddy Walter to visit Junior in the psychiatric hospital in Terrell, Texas. Usually we would spend the day and then stop off in Dallas on the way back to visit with Aunt Dorothy, one of Junior's sisters. We loved stopping there because she was a fantastic cook. She was married but didn't have any children. Her husband's name was Billie, and we always knew there was something funny about him. Apparently, after he passed away a lot of his secrets were uncovered. Mamma's term for it was "having a little sugar," which was a euphemism for being gay, something people didn't talk about openly back then. It didn't really matter to us, because he loved us and we loved him. To us he was just Uncle Billie.

The one positive thing I felt around Daddy Walter was the sense of being protected. No one would dare mess with us with him around. I found out years later that it was rumoured Daddy Walter actually killed a man.

There was a gentle side to Daddy Walter. Every Christmas he would make sure we had a turkey and some groceries. When we lived in Gainesville he used to come Christmas morning and would always bring fresh sausages, which Mamma would cook for breakfast. We would all sit down at the table to eat and listen to Daddy Walter tell us about work and the cows he owned.

Daddy Walter was a man's man, strong and fearless, I liked his confidence. It gave our family and me a sense of protection and strength. He always had a nice car, and it was at all times clean. He used to drive Mamma and us kids to the Goodwill store, where he would buy school clothes for all of us. You see, in reality he was like a lot of us who put on a big tough facade to keep people from getting too close, for fear of getting hurt.

He and Junior were the first black people I knew to have a television. We used to go to their house on Sunday evenings to watch the *Wonderful World of Disney*. That was a big treat.

The next closest thing to a father was my mother's only brother, a man we called Uncle Beji. When we were kids, he worked as an insurance salesman. He was smart and regimented and apparently had gone to college. He was always neatly dressed with a shirt and tie and shoes that shone brightly.

The other thing I remember about Uncle Beji is the discipline he administered with his belt. That was memorable and obviously painful, not because it was excessive or undeserved, but because one of his arms was paralyzed and his hand was deformed. How he could hold one of us with that arm and strap us with the other was a mystery.

Uncle Beji gave me my first job when I was five years old. Every Saturday morning he would take us with him to clean the church. We would dust, sweep and pick up garbage. He would always give us each a shiny dime, which we would put in our piggy banks until the Christmas holidays. Just before Christmas, he would let us break open those little banks and use the money to buy presents.

Our experience with surrogate fathers and the men in Mamma's life didn't end with Uncle Beji. There was Ernest, whom Mamma met when I was around eleven. Ernest was a real country boy who grew up in a hick town called

OUR FATHER: THE PRODIGAL SON RETURNS

Dodge about ten miles from Huntsville. He was short and chunky and had a head full of curly hair.

He was working in Gainesville when he and Mamma met. I remember the night they met because she brought him home to meet us.

"How often I have longed to gather your children together, as a hen gathers her chicks under her wings" (Matthew 23:37 NIV). Mamma was like a mother hen who would have given her life to protect us. She was careful whom she let into the house, so when she allowed Ernest in to come and go as he pleased, we felt we could trust him.

He seemed okay except when he threatened to hit Mamma one time before they were married. Man, no one messed with our mamma. We heard them arguing one night, and we were afraid he might hurt her. We pulled out a butcher knife, a pair of scissors and a skillet from the kitchen drawer and confronted him. "If you hurt our mamma, we will kill you," I said, and he knew we meant business.

Shortly after Ernest moved in with us, he and Mamma were married. They got married at the house. I remember being excited because I was finally going to have my own daddy. However, our excitement was short-lived and turned quickly into fear and anxiety.

Ernest was no doubt the hardest working man I ever met. I had firsthand knowledge of this because on many early mornings I was awakened by the smell of breakfast, which meant it was time to wake up and get ready for work. It got to the point where I hated the smell of eggs because it reminded me of having to get up so early. This was usually around three or four o'clock in the morning.

We did everything from picking cotton, hauling hay and highway construction work to logging and hauling pulpwood. My older brother really resented Ernest. William was the oldest, and I think he felt he had been replaced as the man of the house. He used to tell me how stupid I was for acting like this was our real daddy.

We spent many hot days picking cotton and hauling hay. We were out of the house long before the birds started singing and usually came back home after they had gone back to sleep. We either rode in the back of a pickup truck with other cotton pickers or would be jammed in the front seat of the truck. On top of the back-breaking labour we worked in temperatures well over one hundred degrees plus humidity, with no shade to shield us from the blistering Texas sun.

SEEDS OF FATHERLESSNESS

We thought working in the cotton and hay fields was bad, but compared to working in the woods, it was nothing. While we had plenty of shade in the woods, there was no breeze and the constant danger of being hit by a falling tree or the skidder tractor used to bunch the logs together. Oftentimes it was hard to tell which direction the trees were falling or which way the skidder was coming until the last minute.

I remember William threatening constantly to pour sugar in the gas tank of the truck. One day he decided he wasn't going to work for Ernest one more day. That day, he just up and left. He eventually got a job in town.

Even though I hated the work, it wasn't like Ernest was sending us and staying home; he was there breaking his back trying to make ends meet. He could outwork four men, and man, was he strong! When we used to haul pulpwood, it would sometimes take three men to load a stick of wood on Ernest's shoulder, which he would carry and throw up onto the truck.

I figured any man who would marry a woman with four kids and work so hard to take care of us couldn't be a bad person. To me Ernest was a good man, but I was blinded by my desire for a real daddy. I just figured the added pressure of trying to provide for Mamma and us fuelled a lot of his anger. Even to this day, I truly feel he had good intentions, but his soul was bent.

I remember one day he came home before we left for school and rushed into the house, grabbing the shotgun. Apparently the man he was working for, his first cousin, had cheated him. He was so angry he wanted to kill him. Thank God, Mamma was able to calm him down.

He was very frustrated. One of the ways he would take out his frustrations was at the end of a fan belt from a car or an extension cord, and most of the times I was the target. My most memorable beating was when I was blindfolded with my hands tied behind my back and beaten with a bullwhip because I refused to say I did something I didn't do.

Ernest was sort of like his own boss, even though he paid people like his cousin or ol' man Reiner a healthy cut for using their trucks. He could go and come as he pleased, and he would usually go to the woods before sunup and stay until sundown.

Some of the saddest times with my stepfather were when he had a job in town working nine to five and on the night shift at the bus station. One of us used to take him to dinner when he worked nights, and he would talk about being back in the woods. He seemed so out of place wearing a uniform instead of the overalls he usually wore in the woods. It reminded me of a wild animal caged in a zoo. With Ernest, I experienced firsthand how people in authority use excessive force to control people's behaviour through intimidation and fear.

I remember the first time we were told by our stepfather we would be punished if we received any Cs on our report card. I had some concerns about this because we often had to get up early and go to work before going to school. Most times we were tired. Well the deadline for our first report came and when I opened it, my heart sank. I had four Cs, two Ds and one F.

I was sick to my stomach and had to be excused from school. I remember sitting in the washroom at home trying to figure out what to do. I knew the punishment was four licks with a fan belt for a C, so that meant 16 licks. I figured if he doubled that for the Ds and for the F, I would be dead.

I decided to change the Ds to Cs and the F to an A. That was one of the longest days of my life, waiting for him to come home from work. I lost count of the licks, but I know it was more than 16. I was sore for days after that whipping; however, I only received As and Bs after that. I didn't get good grades because I wanted to please my stepfather but because I wanted to escape his wrath.

White people in the southern United States in the 50s used similar tactics to intimidate us black people. They laid down the laws of segregation, and if we crossed the line we would be beaten up, put in jail or even killed. Some examples were being forced to drink from separate drinking water fountains marked "Colored Only," being told to ride in the back of the bus and only being allowed to eat at the back of restaurants. Although these rules were wrong, they were vigorously enforced.

As crazy as it sounds I actually believed Ernest cared about me, and many of the beatings were provoked out of anger and frustration. I believe he loved us in his own strange way, but like many men who were shown little or no affection by their own fathers, he just didn't know how to show it. Make no mistake though—the white people beating us up, putting us in jail, lynching or shooting us weren't doing it out of love.

I do remember there were times when he would come and sit on the edge of the bed before it was time to wake me up to go to work. I often wondered what he was thinking about as he sat there. He never said anything, and I would pretend to be asleep, hoping he would decide not to get me up to go to work.

However, he would shake my foot real gently and say in a soft tone, "Son, it's time to get up," not wanting to wake up my little brother, Dwight.

I remember several times wanting to hug him, but it was difficult because he just wasn't very receptive. I believe the main reason I never hated him is because I thought he meant well, but most of all I really wanted a father, and as a result I projected him into being my father. In reality, this was a romanticized view of what actually was happening.

I realize now that even though I didn't hate or even resent Ernest, his behaviour toward me had a negative impact on my behaviour toward people, especially those in authority.

One of the worst fears I had as a kid growing up without a father was that my mother or grandmother would die and leave me all alone. I had an even greater fear that my friends would find out that big bad Bruce was actually afraid of being alone. So like many kids I hid my fears by pretending to be a big tough guy. Many kids who are bullies like I was are merely angry and frustrated and are covering up their own fears by pretending to be tough.

This is a classic example of fear of abandonment brought on by a lack of security because of having only one parent. The covering up by pretending to be tough is brought on by shame and pride. After all, I was big for my age and often played football with kids much older than me. I had a reputation to uphold.

One of our favourite games growing up was playing hide and seek. I had a special place I would hide and would often just sit staring up into the sky, crying and pleading with God that whatever He did, He wouldn't let my Mamma or my grandmother, Junior, die before me. I just couldn't bear the thought of being left alone or abandoned.

So like Daddy Walter I developed this mean look and demeanour to keep anyone from getting too close to me for fear of getting hurt. As a result of hiding my real fears, which are really emotions connected to painful events, I became angry, aggressive and abusive, all in an attempt to hide my feelings of insecurity.

I think the best thing Ernest did for me was to move us from Gainesville to Huntsville, Texas, which I know when looking back was the hand of God.

SOME THINGS YOU JUST KNOW

As long as I can remember, I always wanted attention. I know now this is a need for acceptance and approval. When a child realizes he is not wanted by his parents and feels rejected, he is not equipped to deal with these feelings. Even though children may not be able to communicate how they feel, they begin to express their feelings through their behaviour. Some children who are rejected withdraw and become shy and even depressed, while others become aggressive and controlling. I was a little of both.

OUR FATHER: THE PRODIGAL SON RETURNS

According to Mamma, I was a very clingy child. I believe this is because I longed for affection and security. To give us all the attention we needed must have been particularly hard for Mamma because there were four of us born within less than four years. I ended up right in the middle. It shouldn't be hard to figure out who got the least attention, with one sister only 12 months older than me and a brother only 13 months younger.

I craved attention, and one of the ways I got it was by fighting. I didn't care who it was. I even remember fighting with Debra Manual, the same girl I showed my unmentionables to when I was younger. I remember bullying other kids, including Roger, my best friend, by the time I was in the first grade. I also got into many fights as a kid, including one with Roger, who managed somehow to get the best of me. Then there was Ira, who lived next to my grandmother. He was two years older than me. We got into a fight while playing at recess. The teacher decided since I liked fighting so much to put boxing gloves on us. That was my first official boxing match, which I easily won. Beating up a kid older than me made other kids think I was tough and made me feel very important.

My need to control and dominate, I think, was really a desire for acceptance. In those bullying years, the seeds of my fatherlessness were starting to bear fruit.

Men, you think you're only sowing wild oats
When you're out planting seed
But you're producing another generation
That has some real needs.
A need for nurturing
For love and affection
A need for discipline
Guidance and direction
A need for security
Provision and protection too
Some of these needs
Can only be met by you.

SIX

THE ALLEY

Because strait is the gate, and narrow is the way, which leadeth unto life, and few there be that find it (Matthew 7:14 KJV).

We moved to Huntsville in 1961. I was excited to leave Gainesville. I was hoping things would be a whole lot better for us than they had been. We were finally a complete family with Mamma and a real daddy, not a sugar daddy we called uncle, like so many kids I knew.

By this time my baby sister, Donna Latell Smith, had been born. The good news was Ernest's last name was also Smith. It was nice having the same last name. I always found it so confusing when kids had different last names living in the same house.

I was glad we didn't have to change our last name, because people would just think Ernest was my real father. This was about as likely as people believing my father was Dwight's real daddy. My daddy was well over six feet, and Dwight was way shorter than the rest of us. Ernest, on the other hand, was short and could easily pass as Dwight's daddy, but not mine.

Moving to Huntsville was a chance for a new beginning, a chance to leave behind a lot of bad memories. Little did I know that these bad memories were going with me, packed away in a trunk called denial. I had no idea what Huntsville was like or where we would be living. I was glad we weren't moving way out in the country where Ernest came from.

I remember the day we packed up and left Gainesville. I rode down in an old truck with my stepfather, and the stick shift kept jumping out of gear. My job was to hold the stick so it wouldn't jump out of gear all the way from Gainesville to Huntsville, a five-hour drive.

OUR FATHER: THE PRODIGAL SON RETURNS

We finally arrived and drove up in this place appropriately named The Alley. I would live there until I left for university. There was only one way into The Alley and one way out, on a gravel road that doubled as a driveway and a playground.

You must be kidding! This is it? I thought. I didn't even want to unload the truck.

The Alley was a long narrow pathway that became an even narrower trail just past our house. Once you passed our house, the only way to the other houses in The Alley was through this narrow trail.

All the houses in The Alley were rentals, and Dr. Johnson, the only black dentist in town, owned them. In fact, they called it the Johnson addition even though the Doc lived not far from the prison in a nice little brick house that he no doubt owned.

Meanwhile, the houses in The Alley were not much more than wood shacks. Not many people in The Alley owned cars, and it was just as well, because it wouldn't take much to create a traffic jam. There was barely enough room for the people, let alone a bunch of cars. There wasn't even enough room for two cars to pass through at the same time. There were houses on both sides of The Alley and barely enough room to park. Maybe ten families were living in The Alley, and of the ten, only two had fathers, including Ernest, who was really only our stepfather.

Living in The Alley was like living in one of the cellblocks in the state pen, which hovered on our horizon.

Most folks living there had about as much chance of escaping The Alley as a prisoner did escaping "The Walls," which was the term for death row at the prison. The same governmental system running the justice system was in charge of Jim Crow and ensured that the social order would not be changed, at least at that time.

Even though we were not locked up, we were restricted by the colour of our skin and could very easily face a similar fate as a rebellious convict if we got out of line.

In other ways, living in The Alley was like being a wild animal in a zoo. You couldn't sneeze without someone knowing your business. We were like animals in another way, and that is, black fathers were quickly becoming an endangered species.

Our house had only two bedrooms, which meant the four of us were sleeping in the same bedroom, plus now there was a new addition to the family, baby Donna. Two of us slept in bunk beds, and there were two single beds in the room.

We had always been close as kids growing up without a father. We looked after each other and after Mamma. Even though I was the tallest, I always looked up to William as my big brother.

I was envious of William because he was considered the better looking of the two of us and he could easily fit into the second-hand clothes Mamma brought home. Mamma seemed to favour William. Even when we played football against each other I would hold back because I was so much stronger than he was.

Then there was Dwight, my youngest brother. He was much shorter than the rest of us, but we never thought much of it. Ernest did cut him some slack when it came to work and dishing out some of his beatings, and I was glad because of Dwight's size. He really looked up to me. He was like my personal mascot. He was two years younger, which meant at one time we went to different schools. However, Mr. Magee, my high school football coach, would let Dwight in the dressing room before games and even let him travel with us on the bus to our away games.

Our next-door neighbour was a woman we called Ma Dear whose real name was Aretha Sowells. She was a single mom who had four children, three girls and one boy. She was divorced from her children's father, who was an alcoholic. Ma Dear was about the same height as Mamma and had the same complexion, and they both had a couple of gold front teeth.

Ma Dear was very popular with men and had several calling on her. She was very friendly and funny. She was way more outgoing than Mamma. She was real spunky and didn't take crap from anyone. Ma Dear could cut you down with a flick of her sharp tongue. She was good for Mamma because Mamma was a little uptight.

We became close friends with the whole family. The oldest was a girl, Willie Lee, then Faye, then Dick, who would become my best friend, and then Linda, whom we called Punkin. Across from them was a girl called Martha Faye, who lived with her mother and her brother, Buddy. Buddy would eventually get Punkin pregnant, and they had a son.

Mamma and Ma Dear became best friends. They made sure there was always something for all of us to eat. I used to love hanging out at Dick's house, and I always had a crush on one sister or another. Man, that Ma Dear was funny, and we were just like one of the family.

Then there was Miss Clara. She had five kids by two different men and no husband at the time. I guess she was what you might call a black widow, because she always had men way younger than her shacking up with her.

Across from us were Geneva Shaw and her brother, who lived with their mother and no father.

Clarence was a black Creole from Louisiana. Man, his skin was the colour of coal, and he spoke some weird language. I now realize it was French Creole patois. He and his wife had ten kids, and we used to think they were all crazy. They were actually nice people, just different than the rest of us. Two of his sons, Leander and Clarence Jr., whom we called Shine because he was so black, were always in trouble.

Other than Dick and his family, we were never really close to any of the families in The Alley. All of my other close friends lived elsewhere in Huntsville. You couldn't come or go in The Alley without someone seeing you.

Life in The Alley was routine except when we had to get up early to go to work and get back in time for school. We usually slept in until about eight o'clock, got up, then dressed and met friends to walk to school. I don't remember having breakfast. Most of the kids ate lunch in the cafeteria. A few of us stayed outside; we were either embarrassed because we had no lunch or even more embarrassed because of what we had for lunch. I remember pretending many times not to be hungry because I didn't have any lunch. One lunchtime, I hid in the closet in my classroom because I was so embarrassed about what I brought for lunch. It was one of Mamma's Spam sandwiches, and in my mind only poor people ate Spam.

One of my first new friends in the sixth grade was a kid name L. A. Oliphant. He broke his arm one semester and had to wear a cast. We always hung out together, so he wanted me to have lunch with him, but I couldn't afford to eat in the cafeteria. I don't know whose idea it was, but he told me his parents would give me lunch money every day if I carried his tray for him.

I was more than willing, because eating in the cafeteria meant I was as good as the other kids. I must admit I often wondered if the other kids knew of this, because if they did, I would have been even more ashamed.

My other friend was a kid called Pop. He was real dark with eyes that seemed to pop out of his head. Pop lived in a part of town called the new addition. I don't know why they called it that, because there wasn't anything new about it, mostly old rundown houses like the ones in The Alley. I loved going to his house to play because he lived close to an old creek, where we would spend hours craw fishing. This was before Dick and his family moved into The Alley, right next door to us. After they moved in Dick and I were inseparable. Even after I beat him up one time after arguing while playing football, we remained best friends.

Our house in The Alley wasn't much to look at, but we had one of the biggest backyards. Our porch overlooked the yard, where we handwashed our clothes using a scrub board and lye soap. A little creek we called The Branch trickled just behind the house. We used to fish there for crawfish and sail home-made boats. On the other side of The Branch was little Mount Olive, the Methodist church we attended.

We had good friends who lived right next door to the church. The woman's name was Miss Mayzella. She had five kids and no husband. They were Mack Wendel Jr., his brother, whom we called "baby brother," and three sisters who were what folks called high yellow because of their light complexions.

Ms. Mayzella ended up marrying a man called Broomfield. He had actually come to our church to hold revival meetings. He called himself a prophet. I don't know if he was really a prophet, but he could sure do miracles on racoons and possums. He apparently even cooked up skunk.

When we moved to Huntsville, I was going into the sixth grade. We had to walk all the way across town to attend school in Rogersville. It was a way nicer school than the one we attended in Gainesville. The one thing we did as kids in school in Gainesville and Huntsville was start the morning pledging our allegiance to the flag, singing "The Star Spangled Banner" and reciting the Lord's Prayer. Even though we recited these things with our mouths, our hearts weren't really in it, because we knew we were not considered equal to our white counterparts who recited the same things.

Rogersville was also a much nicer part of town than where we lived in The Alley. The black people living there seemed to be a lot better off than we were. The streets were paved and the houses looked well built.

I found out that in the mid-1800s there were prominent blacks living in Huntsville who came there before the Civil War and settled in Rogersville. Unbelievably, many of them were members of predominately white churches.

In 1867, black Methodists and Baptists built their own churches. The Baptists established the first Baptist church in Rogersville, which is still there to this day. Evidently, this is where these prominent blacks bought homes. This explains why Rogersville was a higher class neighbourhood. It is hard to imagine this actually happened, because there were no signs blacks and whites had actually attended church together or mixed at all. If you were black living in Huntsville, you knew your place, and it definitely was at the back of the bus, as far as whites were concerned.

The one thing I liked about our house in The Alley was the trees. We had lots of them. This was great because they provided cover to play hide and seek and when we pretended we were soldiers in an army or cowboys and Indians.

We had a fig tree, an old magnolia tree and a number of pecan trees. I enjoyed just being able to pick and eat the pecans, but I hated it when fall came because it meant constantly having to rake up all those leaves.

Our backyard would become the place of many memorable basketball games. We often played well past daylight. It was far from anything fancy. We had this hoop attached to a rickety wood backboard, which was nailed to one of the trees, and the surface was a well-worn dirt area where there had once been some grass.

Playing football on gravel in The Alley in Huntsville is where I developed a real passion and skill for the game. It was a long narrow stretch, so deking people out was a skill I developed at a young age. We always played tackle football, whether on gravel pavement or the hard ground. So learning how to avoid would-be tacklers was also a way to avoid scrapes and cuts.

Dick and I spent hours playing football against each other, just working on our moves and talking about making our school team. I enjoyed playing outside, but I lived to play football.

We would often meet up with several kids to walk to school every day. I went to high school in the seventh grade because we didn't have a junior school when we first moved to Huntsville. Our normal route to school then was along the main road that ran all the way from town past our school.

Occasionally if we were late we would take a shortcut through the white neighbourhood. I'll never forget one time we took the shortcut, and this little white girl, maybe three years old, ran out on the front porch and screamed, "Mommy, Mommy, look at those niggers!"

Church was walking distance from The Alley, as well as Ms. Modeen's corner store, where we often went to buy groceries and treats. Ms. Modeen looked like she was mixed. She was light brown with wavy hair, kind of tall and heavy set, and she was very hairy, even having a light moustache. She was always nice and polite and never made me feel unwelcome, even sometimes giving me a free ice cream cone. She had three kids, but she was divorced from their father, who owned the funeral home right next door.

THE ALLEY

Miss Modeen lived above her store, and her ex-husband lived next door to the funeral home. William became good friends with the oldest boy, R. L. Jr. He would even go in the back of the funeral home where they embalmed the dead bodies. They would invite us to come in sometimes, but I was horrified of dead bodies.

After living in The Alley for a while my stepfather arranged to have credit at her store. I remember there were times when he would go for months and not pay her. This was real embarrassing, because we were friends with her kids. I hated it when Mamma would send me there to get something on credit. I would never go up to the counter if there was anyone else in the store. I was always afraid she would embarrass me by saying no, because the bill hadn't been paid.

My stepfather had a similar arrangement with the local barber. I always felt so proud when I went in and had money to pay the man at the end of the month. However, there were other times when I knew my stepfather hadn't paid in a while. When this happened I would always let everyone go before me, often waiting hours until the place emptied. I couldn't take a chance that he would say no and embarrass me in front of everyone.

I felt so ashamed that people knew how poor we were. We never seemed to have money for anything. We weren't on welfare, but it sure felt like it. I think for the most part we were actually better off than many of the people living in The Alley. We at least had food in the house most of the time.

In Huntsville, there wasn't much to do. The most excitement we had was when people would come there for the Texas Prison Rodeo. The town would fill up with folks for it every year. The people who lived there lived for the rodeo because they could charge lots of money for parking. We were walking distance from the prison but not close enough to make extra cash parking cars, and even if we had been, there was no room in The Alley to park a lot of cars.

The prison was the biggest building in Huntsville next to the local college, Sam Houston State College. We were close enough to the prison to hear the alarm when someone tried to escape. Whenever we had to walk close to the prison, you couldn't help but notice the white prison guards, heavily armed, usually wearing dark glasses, like the guard "The Man With No Eyes" who wore mirrored shades in the movie *Cool Hand Luke*. From all accounts, life in there wasn't much better than what that movie described. The Huntsville State Prison was a maximum-security prison that electrocuted men on death row. The death row inmates were housed in a section called "The Walls," which exists to this day. All executions in the State of Texas, which has always led the U.S. in executing prisoners, were carried out at the prison. During the years I was there, at least until 1964, the method of final deliverance was electrocution.

The infamous chair at Huntsville was called "Old Sparky," and living within walking distance of this bastion of ultimate law enforcement was sobering. The chair was called "Old Sparky" because the strength of the electrical flow sometimes caused sparks to actually fly off the executed as they faced their earthly demise. Late at night whenever the lights would flicker we would say, "Someone must be in that old electric chair."

We had a local theatre and a Dairy Queen, but they were segregated, with a separate entrance and a section in the balcony for the blacks and a window at the back of the Dairy Queen where we had to order. Going to the high school football games, though, was a big treat. We loved watching our team, the Huntsville High Tigers. When I was in the sixth and seventh grade, our heroes were Burt Reed and Robert Holmes, whom we called Dough Belly. They were in the same backfield and both ended up getting football scholarships to Southern University in Baton Rouge. Dough Belly later went pro with the Kansas City Chiefs and actually made rookie of the year, later playing in the Super Bowl.

Cooke County was dry, meaning you couldn't buy liquor there. As a result, we had "booze cans" where people would go to dance and drink beer and get "chalk," which was homemade liquor. It wasn't unusual for someone we knew to get knifed or shot to death, like Murray Tucker, one of my brother's best friends.

Murray had just come from a second stint in Vietnam, and he and William had gone to one of these booze cans. According to William, he and Murray were sitting at the bar, and as they got up to leave some guy accidentally stepped on Murray's foot. Murray apparently threatened this guy, but before he could carry out his threat, the guy pulled out a gun and shot him in the head.

When people wanted the real thing to drink they would drive over the Trinity River, about a twenty-minute drive into the next county, where they could buy beer, wine or hard liquor. I remember my stepfather dropping men off at booze cans after work on Friday. Sometime he would go in for a couple of beers. On a couple of occasions, I would get out of the truck and peek through the window. Most of these places were nothing more than a one-room shack; however, they were packed with black folks drinking, dancing, laughing and letting it all hang out. I couldn't wait until I was old enough to go to one of these places.

THE ALLEY

Things were quiet in The Alley, mainly because there was no through traffic, and unless you lived there or were visiting someone there was no other reason to be there except to play basketball or football. The most excitement in The Alley was when Clarence got drunk and beat his wife or one of his kids, which was usually on the weekends.

One day we came home from school, and the house right across The Alley from us almost burned down. The woman living there was a single mother and unfortunately had gone out and left small kids unattended. The firemen tried frantically to rescue them, but they had huddled in a closet to get away from the fire and were lost. That's not something you ever forget.

I remember being in the ninth grade when John F. Kennedy was president. He was real popular with black people. This was around the time Russia was attempting to set up a nuclear base in Cuba, creating a threat of World War III. We waited all tense as President Kennedy refused to back down from the Russian president, Nikita Khrushchev. The unthinkable happened in 1963 right in Dallas. The president was assassinated.

I was ashamed to be from Texas. Although the Warren Commission ruled the killing was the work of a crazed gunman, Lee Harvey Oswald, many believe the president was targeted because of the federal government's efforts to end segregation and allow blacks to fully integrate into Texas schools, workplaces and throughout society.

OF DEATH ROW, JIM CROW AND MINSTREL SHOWS

Things were really heating up on the civil rights scene. It was around this time that popular civil rights activist Medgar Evers was murdered. Three young civil rights activists, two white and one black, were also missing and presumed murdered in Mississippi. Later this was confirmed.

It was a time in America when the southern states operated under Jim Crow laws, brought in after the Civil War when the slaves were "freed." However, the white folks in the south, while begrudgingly realizing they no longer could enslave blacks, did not want them living next to whites as equals, so they set up a whole system of segregation of the races to ensure their position in society could not be challenged.

They called them "Jim Crow" laws after a character in a 19th century minstrel show, a clear sign of white America's lack of respect for the black man. The Jim Crow character was a stereotypical poor, uneducated, "shiftin' and shuffling" southern black who was popularized by a white performer from England called Daddy Rice. Rice, an English immigrant, created this character around 1828, when he came up with the concept of blackface, an act where whites put on black makeup to simulate blacks. In these minstrel shows, the buffoon-like antics of poor, woebegone "Negroes," entertained whites. The character was so popular it became the symbol for the laws enacted across the U.S. after the Civil War, which were designed to ensure blacks were "equal but separate." In Gainesville, we were definitely separate but in no way equal.

I find it strange in retrospect that those "humorous" minstrel shows that I snuck into as a kid back in Gainesville were actually the basis for social policy in the southern states. They always started late at night. According to Mamma, this kind of stuff was off limits to us. I remember we crawled under the tent one night and saw people doing what they called dirty dancing, which kids would call dignified today.

There were stand-up comics who wore outrageous outfits like Flavor Flav, the rapper of today. They swore and told dirty jokes as part of the night's entertainment. It seemed like harmless fun. We were too young to realize the images from the minstrel show were created by white people to heap scorn on black people with their characterization of us as shiftless, lazy, stupid and sex-crazed.

Reminders we weren't equal were everywhere and included statues of the Jim Crow character on white people's lawns. It didn't matter how old you were or what the name on your birth certificate said, to most white people your name was "Boy."

We were taught in school that President Abraham Lincoln had emancipated us after many people, black and white, died fighting in the Civil War to abolish slavery. However, this man from England had managed to promote the notion of white supremacy under the guise of entertainment.

Although slavery was abolished and the Declaration of Independence stated, "We hold these truths to be self-evident, that all men are created equal, that they are endowed by their Creator with certain unalienable rights, that among these are life, liberty and the pursuit of happiness," it was evident that we were not treated as equals. We couldn't live anywhere we wanted and at times had no right even to live, and we were often pursued and even hanged for sport. We couldn't even be buried where we wanted.

On top of that, we had no real visible role models other than entertainers, many of whom had bleached skin and processed hair, or schoolteachers who were considered inferior to their white counterparts. A handful of famous athletes were also icons for us but for the most part were not accessible.

For many of us the most visible role models were men who had numerous children by different women or pimps with loud-coloured clothes, big fancy hats and large flashy cars. We see the same thing today with many of the rap stars called gangstas, who in my opinion are just putting on another form of minstrel show, depicting black men as pimps and black women as whores.

When I was a kid, on television there was *Our Gang* with Buckwheat and Stymie; old Amos and his sidekick Andy; Rochester, the butler on the *Jack Benny* Program; and the movie *Cabin in the Sky*. All of them reinforced the images projected by the Jim Crow character. We were lazy, ignorant, singing and dancing Negroes, happy with our place in society, was the pervasive and constant television message. However, if you listen closely to the words of many of the songs— the blues, and especially those referred to as old Negro spirituals—these are not words of happy people but people who are deeply hurt and in pain.

The pain comes from burdens too heavy to bear, from the legacies of slavery, one of the most tragic of which is the breakdown of the black family as a result of centuries of the emasculation of the black man and the sexual exploitation of the black woman. It was this kind of legacy that spawned the birth of groups like the NAACP, which began to rise in popularity in the early and mid-sixties with leaders like Dr. Martin Luther King Jr. and Mr. Ralph Abernathy. Their names were on everybody's lips in black communities across America.

Change was in the wind, and the winds of change were blowing toward Texas. In 1966, we knew things were going to be different when a group of white and black civil rights activists showed up in our town. They set up shop across the road from The Alley, started having meetings and began to recruit members.

Word got out real fast that there were some white folk from up north saying some scary and exciting stuff. The sign on the door said "Hey You," and when I saw that sign I knew they meant me.

Our new freedom song was "We Shall Overcome." Even though that day seemed a long way off, things were about to heat up in Huntsville. Soon they had us marching with signs all over town, singing that song. For us this was exciting, especially when we would skip class to picket.

I'll never forget when they convinced us to sit at the counter at an all-white greasy spoon. A bunch of us went in and sat down right where they told us. Man, if looks could kill. The cook came out with a big knife in his hand and a mean look on his face. We took a deep breath and ordered. "Four hamburgers with french fries, please."

"We don't serve niggers in here!" was the reply.

Without a moment's hesitation I jumped in. "We didn't order niggers; we ordered a hamburger with french fries."

He refused to serve us, so we got up and left.

Things finally came to a head, and Texas was forced to integrate. Then life got real strange in Huntsville.

Jim Crow was more than a comedy act
Jim Crow was an attitude towards blacks
It said, you are less than white folks
And your place is in the back.
It said, you're not as smart
And not nearly as bright
And the difference is
As drastic as day and night.
Jim Crow meant you'd better behave
Because through white eyes
You were still a slave!

SEVEN

THE SON RISES

*My son, pay attention to my wisdom, listen well to
my words of insight* (Proverbs 5:1 NIV).

I wanted a father so much that I often tried to rationalize why my stepfather, Ernest, was the way he was. I would come up with all these different reasons why my real father didn't stick around. It was easier to make up excuses
than to face the reality that our real father had abandoned us and our stepfather
was abusing us.

Although Ernest abused us, there were some fun times. The most memorable were when he and I huddled in front of the TV set watching our favourite
football team. Ever since I was "knee high to a duck," I loved playing football.
I started playing pickup football and baseball at five. We played everywhere, on
the side of the house, on the streets, in The Alley and on the field at school.

I knew what I wanted to do when I grew up and often daydreamed about
what it would be like to play professional football. I got my chance to tell my
whole class one day when the teacher asked each of us what we wanted to do
when we grew up.

"When I grow up I am going to be a professional football player," I
shouted.

My favourite team was the Cleveland Browns, and my favourite player was
big Jim Brown, number 32. Right after watching them play I would go outside
and pretend to be Brown, even copying his walk back to the huddle.

My stepfather liked Brown too, but his favourite player was number 42,
Paul Warfield. My fondest memory of my stepfather is when we watched football together after church on Sundays, especially if the Browns were playing. He
used to laugh when Jim Brown would get up after being tackled and walk slowly

OUR FATHER: THE PRODIGAL SON RETURNS

back to the huddle as if he was hurt or tired. Then, on the very next play, bam! Brown would slash off tackle, breaking would-be challengers and running over others as he took the ball to the house into the end zone.

My stepfather would go nuts laughing so hard. I loved it when he laughed. He was like a little kid then.

His favourite team was the old Baltimore Colts. His favourite quarterback was number 19, Johnny Unitas, and his favourite player was number 24, Lenny Moore. We would hardly ever miss a game, and that meant a lot to me. I always looked forward to Sunday, and to be honest it wasn't because of church but because it meant watching football with my stepfather.

The other thing I remember is going to church and having dinner as a family when my stepfather was there. He forbade us from playing football on Sundays, but one Sunday I sneaked off for a game. In the midst of it, I broke free, leaped up to make a flying catch and landed on top of a post, mouth first. That's how I lost my two front teeth.

They weren't knocked out completely but dangled from the roof of my mouth. Instead of taking me to the dentist, they took me to the hospital, and by the time a dentist saw me, it was too late to save the teeth. There was only one black dentist in town, but we never saw him unless we had a toothache. Every time I would go there, I would come home with fewer teeth.

Another thing we did as kids was go to the local fair every summer. Ernest would give us all a couple of dollars to go on rides and play some games. My favourite ride was the Ferris Wheel, and sometimes he would ride it with us. We also loved going in the funhouse with those weird mirrors. When I was a little older, he would let us help tear down the rides to earn some extra dough, which we were allowed to keep.

I think Ernest really tried, but he just wasn't equipped to deal with leading a ready-made family. Like a lot of men, he had walked out of a marriage, leaving two kids of his own that by all accounts were screwed up.

I realize now that, even though I didn't hate or even resent Ernest, his behaviour toward me had a negative impact on my behaviour later on.

One thing I did resent was having to work so hard. I worked like a slave and didn't get paid. Some of the men who worked with us used to feel sorry for me. Several times they secretly slipped me a couple of bucks.

Even though Ernest called me son, to be honest I never felt like a son, but more like a slave, a hired hand who never got paid. Old Man River had nothing on me. He only sang about toting that barge and lifting that bail. I actually did it and had the proof, with a callous on my shoulder so hard you couldn't penetrate it with a knife. I still have some of the scratches and scars as reminders today.

I do remember getting paid one time. I got 20 cents. I spent it going swimming in the local pool before the city closed it down because they didn't want us swimming with white people. My stepfather tore a strip off my behind for spending that money going swimming.

The worst summer I ever had was when I was fourteen. As soon as school was out for the summer, I was shipped off to Ernest's father out in the country. There was no television and no indoor toilets, which meant doing the do in an outhouse. It was like living this long nightmare. There was one highlight living there, and that was Aunt Nell. She was fine and real funny. I had a huge crush on her.

She was living there with her husband, and I would lie awake listening to them making out. I was fourteen, and you can imagine what was going on in my head. Unfortunately, by the time I left university, she had lost her mind and was no longer capable of taking care of herself.

I worked like a dog that summer, lifting heavy pulpwood with my step-grandfather while his younger son, George, got to drive the truck. Grandpa Smith was getting up in age and couldn't lift heavy loads, so I did most of the heavy lifting.

I would get to come home on Saturdays after working all week so I could be home on Sundays to go to church and have Sunday dinner. At least I got paid that summer. I earned twelve dollars. I used the money to buy some school clothes and to go to the movies a couple of times.

I didn't realize it until later, but this really affected my attitude towards work. I was always a good worker and took pride in doing things well. However, I noticed from time to time I would slack off and excuse myself because of how hard I had to work as a kid. It's like I was trying to make up for all the times I had to work while most of my friends got to stay home and watch cartoons or play football or something else.

Then there were the times when we had to go right through town carrying a load of pulpwood. Oftentimes I would have to ride on the outside on top of the load, where everyone could see me. I felt so ashamed and embarrassed, especially if someone I knew saw me. To make matters worse, I was sweet on the daughter of the man who owned the truck we were using, and this just wasn't cool.

OUR FATHER: THE PRODIGAL SON RETURNS

While I was scarred on the outside from the scratches and cuts from working in the woods, I was bruised on the inside from the abuse, the lack of love and affection, plus the shame. While scratches mar your body and leave flesh wounds, emotional bruising scars your soul and leaves you with a wounded spirit. The payoff was that I became extremely strong from all the hard work.

The thing that amazed people, including coaches, players, men and women, were my arms. Trimming those large branches from giant trees developed arms that guys who lifted weights for years would die for. People called my arms everything from tree trunks to elephant stumps, from tree limbs to legs hanging from my shoulders. However, the name that stuck with me was Paul Bunyan.

Paul Bunyan was a mythical American lumberjack who had a pet ox and carried a big axe. Legend said it was big enough and he was strong enough to cut down even trees like giant red oaks and great cedars. People have made monuments of these trees, created songs about them, even produced little statues folks take home to show off to friends, neighbours and relatives.

I even sometimes wore bib overhauls like Bunyan's. People would see me coming and say, "There goes Paul Bunyan," or "Bruce, you're as strong as ole Paul Bunyan's ox."

Rather than cutting me down like some of the other comments, these built me up. Unfortunately they eventually puffed me up until I found myself staring at my giant biceps in the mirror, wondering if I could make some extra scratch by charging people to touch them or letting them take a picture of me.

While my stepfather went a bit overboard, taking us out of Gainesville would help me find my destiny. The hard work saved me from having to slave for years in the gym to get the body and the arms that made me a bull on the football field. Eventually this strength would help me become a "spiritual" Paul Bunyan, ploughing the fields of Christ's harvest like an ox pulling a wagon.

So I thank God for Ernest, my stepfather, who left a mark that has become part of a positive inheritance for me and others like me.

LOOKING BACK

When I was growing up, if you wanted to pick a fight with someone of dark skin, all you had to do was call them black. There were many negative stereotypes perpetuated about blacks. We were called Negroes or coloured by liberal-thinking whites, but most whites called us everything including spook, coon, nigger, and of course the favourite of most white people where I grew up, "boy."

THE SON RISES

There was not much to be proud of as a black kid growing up. There was no sense of history or purpose. There were no positive role models on TV, only blacks playing roles as butlers or maids and others made to look like idiots and Stepin Fetchit fools like Amos and Andy.

There was no black history month, even though there were several black history makers like George Washington Carver and Booker T. Washington. The impression we got from the textbooks was that blacks were an inferior race of people who were created to be subservient to whites, who were superior. The environment in which we grew up also reinforced this.

The ugly reality of being black in America was driven home one day when my stepfather stopped by a convenience store that sold gas. It was owned by a white man who also owned the truck my stepfather drove. We stopped to gas up and pick up a few things for lunch. I was about fifteen. The old man who owned the store was talking to a couple of white men when we came in, and you could tell they were talking about us.

Shortly after we entered the old man who owned the store turned and pointed his finger at my stepfather and said to the other two men, "That's my nigger!" and my stepfather meekly nodded. I was so mad and humiliated.

"Why would you take that from that old cracker?" I cried. Being called black was a bigger problem for my older sister, Peggy, because she was darker than the rest of us. However, what I was ashamed of most was my lips.

If someone really wanted to hurt me or pick a fight with me, they just had to make fun of my lips. I heard every name in the book, including liver lips, lips like tires, tube lips and flapjacks. In most pictures of me as a teen, I had my lips tucked in to make them look smaller. Now big lips are in vogue and white people are paying thousands of dollars to get lips that look like mine.

Not only was I ashamed because of the kind of work we had to do—picking cotton and going to work riding in the back of someone's pickup truck—I was also ashamed being around the kids whose mamma had stolen our father. This was embarrassing as well as humiliating.

This also worked in reverse, I felt ashamed the few times I was around my stepfather's kids because they probably felt the same way as I did, that we had stolen their father.

There is no question that not having a loving father or father figure and feeling rejected were major causes of my low self-esteem. For me and many other black people, we faced rejection, not only from our absentee fathers, but from the social stereotyping of blacks. As a black boy growing up in the south, the seeds were planted for later understanding how much my people and I needed to overcome.

> *I hid my shame with pride*
> *I hid my pain with lies*
> *And before I left The Alley*
> *The rage burned inside.*

EIGHT

UNCLE LEO

And Laban said to [Jacob], "Surely you are my bone and my flesh."
And he stayed with him for a month (Genesis 29:14 NKJV).

Most of my friends looked forward to the end of the school year and the summer break. I didn't, because it meant backbreaking work in the woods with my stepfather or his father for little or no pay.

However, the summer of 1966 would be like no other. My real father was from a very large family. While growing up in Gainesville, we met several of his brothers and one of his sisters, my favourite aunt on his side, Aunt Sally.

Two of my father's brothers lived in Dallas, which was about a forty-five minute drive from Gainesville. We had relatives from both sides of the family living in Dallas.

From time to time while living in Gainesville we would visit some of our relatives, usually on Mamma's side. Once while visiting in Dallas, Daddy Walter took us to visit one of my father's brothers, Uncle Leo. We met Uncle Leo and his wife, Daisy, at their business. They were like people you might see in feature stories on successful and prominent blacks in *Ebony* or *Jet* magazine. I had read stories about people like that but never dreamed I was actually related to any of them.

Called "prominent Negroes," they were educated, refined and prosperous. Many people believe that all black people living in America at this time were poor, living in shacks in the rural south or in urban ghettos of major cities like Harlem in New York or the south side of Chicago, but this was not the case. Uncle Leo and Daisy were both business people and owners of a supermarket, ladies' clothing store and at one time a service station. They had the look of successful people with all the trappings.

OUR FATHER: THE PRODIGAL SON RETURNS

I remember when we walked through the supermarket and the clothing store how proud we were when they would introduce us as their nephews and nieces. My pride turned to awe when we visited their home on Oak Cliff, a street off Oakland Avenue in South Dallas. The street was lined on both sides with large mature trees in what had once been an exclusive white neighbourhood.

I couldn't believe my eyes. This was the biggest house I had ever seen. It was beautiful and made of brown brick and stone, set far back from the street with a long driveway and a well-manicured lawn and many varieties of beautiful flowers.

As impressive as the outside was, the inside was spectacular. It seemed to go on and on, and we had never seen furnishings and decorations like that before. We were like country bumpkins visiting Uncle Jed and Jethro of the Beverley Hillbillies.

On this trip I would meet their one and only child, my first cousin Dardy Glenda. Shortly after meeting us, he took us to see his room. His bedroom was almost as big as our house. He had stuff in his room I hadn't even dreamed of. On top of that, he even had his own bathroom and closets full of clothes. Dardy had his own TV and enough toys to have his own toy store. On top of that, he had a pony.

Uncle Leo and Aunt Daisy had their own boat, which they used to go deep-sea fishing in the Gulf of Mexico. They even had the prize trophy of a blue Marlin stuffed and mounted over the fireplace in the den.

I laughed when Dardy told me how he and Uncle Leo went deep-sea fishing. The only deep-sea fishing I had ever done was fishing for catfish at the bottom of an old dirty pond or crawfish in the creek. We thought Dardy was the luckiest boy in the world, a black Ritchie Rich. All of us left there wishing Uncle Leo and Aunt Daisy would adopt us. However, after we moved to Huntsville it would be a number of years before I saw them again.

I really don't remember how it happened, but in the summer of 1966, my junior year in high school, I had a dream come true. I was invited to spend the summer in Dallas with Uncle Leo, Aunt Daisy and Dardy.

They agreed to help me get a summer job and said I could work and live there. The house had a third floor with three bedrooms. There was one for the housekeeper and one for me, and from time to time my half-sister Jenny lived there. She had a baby and was there finishing school.

It took me a while to settle in, and Aunt Daisy tried hard to make me feel at home. Although she was sophisticated and well educated, she was warm and caring. She would always remind me how important it was to get an education. I would smile and listen and say, "Yes, ma'am."

Uncle Leo was all business, and most of the time I saw him he was wearing a suit and tie. They were real socialites, entertained a lot and often had visits from celebrities at their home. Aunt Daisy would proudly introduce me and say, "This is my nephew Bruce, who is going to go to college to get an education and play football."

Then there was Dardy, who was several years older than me and made sure I knew my place. This was like TV's *Fresh Prince of Bel-Air,* with Dardy being Carlton, the natural son, and me being Will, the "wannabe" son.

Dardy demonstrated an unspoken sense of superiority, which defined our roles. I knew he was the heir and I, the houseboy. If I ever forgot my place, there was always cutting their huge lawn every weekend to remind me. That was my job. I also cleaned, painted and did other odd jobs around the outside of the house.

In fact, it seemed like Dardy hadn't heard that Lincoln had freed the slaves a century earlier. He treated me like his "personal slave." Often he would sit on the front porch sipping on a Coke float while I worked in the hot sun. I didn't mind cutting the lawn or doing the work around the house. I was happy to be there, away from The Alley.

I was up and out of the house by 7:00 a.m. every morning to catch a bus to be at work by 8:00. I was working in construction, building a mausoleum, and often worked twelve-hour days and sometimes a half day on Saturday.

That summer I got to know two of my cousins on my father's side, Beverly Ann and my favourite cousin, Janice. They would pick me up on Saturdays after I finished my chores and let me hang out with them. We had loads of fun.

The other great thing about that summer was getting paid, and it wasn't the 20 cents or the twelve dollars I had made slaving in the hot sun working in the woods with my stepfather and his father. With the money I made I was the best-dressed kid in my senior year, and I had the look and trappings of success.

It's amazing how much of an influence that summer had on me. I had gotten a taste of what it was like to be successful, and I wanted more. After that summer, I knew there was a whole other kind of life outside The Alley, and I wanted it. Even though I was only there for several months, it helped me to believe I could succeed.

It was even harder accepting the way things were after spending the summer in Dallas. It's a whole lot easier to accept something when there is nothing better to compare it to.

OUR FATHER: THE PRODIGAL SON RETURNS

I often hoped in the back of my mind that I could stay there rather than having to go back to The Alley or that at least one day I would receive some kind of inheritance from Uncle Leo and Aunt Daisy, which of course never happened.

When I left Dallas that summer
I wasn't the same
I was thinking different
And expecting change
That summer with Dardy proved
Life wasn't fair
Why wasn't I Uncle Leo's heir?

NINE

TWO, FOUR, SIX, EIGHT,
WE DON'T WANT TO INTEGRATE

"Freedom is never voluntarily given by the oppressor; it must be demanded by the oppressed." (Martin Luther King Jr.)

For us the excitement of integration wasn't about going to school with white kids. We were as nervous to be around them as they were around us. It was the excitement of finally getting to play football against them. We could hardly wait to have the opportunity to legally hit one of them on the field and not go to jail or, worse, be lynched. However, we got the shock of our lives. Rather than being sent to a white school or having a chance to compete against them in football, the unthinkable happened.

They decided to send a white principal to our school, a frail looking man named Mr. Stiles. They also sent a handful of white students, what we called white trash, some Mexicans and, to our shock and amazement, three white coaches. It seemed they sent some of our best students to the white school and some of their worst students to ours. Most of the kids they sent were in courses like auto mechanics or shop. I don't remember any white kids being in any of my classes, and none of them were on the football team.

Little did I know the head coach, this podgy and very nervous white man named Morris Magee, would be instrumental in shaping my life as well as in getting me in shape to become a star in high school football. He was apparently all set to coach at another white school and at the last minute was asked by the district superintendent to take this assignment, coaching a bunch of coloured kids. According to his wife, Frankie Magee, they gave him overnight to think about it, and being a religious man, he prayed.

Well, God must have spoken to him in a dream or something because, according to Mrs. Magee, he felt it was his calling. I am sure he had different thoughts when he met me, because I didn't want to have anything to do with any white coaches, and I let them know right away.

It was a tense time in Huntsville, especially around Sam Houston High, and it would only be a matter of time before things snapped. Civil rights demonstrations were becoming more frequent. Activists from out of town were helping us organize demonstrations in front of restaurants and other public places where blacks were not allowed. A couple of our classmates were arrested for picketing and put in jail. These were friends of ours, so their parents pressured us into boycotting the football team to force the school to bail them out. I felt compelled to lead the boycott.

We would sit in the stands while they were practicing, yelling "Uncle Tom" to the players and black coaches. We decided after a week to come back on the team only to sabotage it by just going through the motions.

We finally had a showdown at halftime in our first game. Our game plan was to not block or tackle anyone and to make Coach Magee and his two white assistant coaches look foolish, hoping they would quit and go back where they came from. We felt bad for the other black assistant coaches, Coach Morris Johnson, Coach Bob Hopkins and Coach Williams, but we felt we had to do it.

Our plan was working. We were down thirty-two to nothing in the first half. You would think we were winning the way we were laughing and carrying on in the locker at halftime. While we were laughing, they were fuming, and their faces were as red as a fire trucks.

In the middle of our little celebration the youngest, Coach Skeeter, picked up a helmet and slammed into one of the lockers. "I know you think you are hurting us, but you're only hurting yourselves. Maybe if I were you I would do the same thing. You can either go back out there and embarrass yourselves and prove everything that white people think and say about you is true, or you can go out and prove you're as good as any white team," he said.

After that speech, we turned our anger toward the other team, coming back in the second half to almost win the game.

We really bonded after that game. Our new coaches started a conditioning program for us and taught us how to become a team. For the remainder of that season we were one of the best teams in our district. In my senior year, we won our district and won the reputation of being one of the finest high school teams in Texas.

Coach Skeeter was also our baseball coach. We had a lot of respect for him, because he was straight up and never disrespected us. He was like a big brother who really cared.

I was a left-handed pitcher and a first baseman, so I needed a right-handed glove for my catching hand. However, since most ball players are right-handed, gloves for left-handers were scarce. On top of that, being poor, all I had was a hand-me-down, like everything else in my universe. It didn't matter to me that I had to wear my left-hand glove on my right hand, because at least I had a glove, which was more than some of the other kids on our team.

One day Coach Skeeter surprised me with a brand new right-handed glove. It was rare that I got anything new. The fact it came from coach Skeeter spoke volumes about him as a person. This glove really meant a lot to me and proved he wasn't just there because it was a job but he really cared about us as people. Not only did he pay for that glove with his own money, he took the time to find a glove for a left-hander.

Coach Magee was also an exceptional guy. A lot more than a coach, he was a father figure who affirmed me as a player and as a person. His wife insisted I was his favourite.

He never talked down to us and always promoted a positive attitude instead of telling us how bad we were. He took an interest in us. For him coaching was about more than just winning ballgames. I found this out one day when he yanked me as the ace pitcher on our school baseball team out of the game because I was throwing at the opposing batters to scare them. After warning me a couple of times, he marched out to the mound and got right up in my face.

By the time the game was over he had cooled off. We sat on the bench and talked about the incident. He told me I was one of the leaders the other kids looked up to, so how I behaved was important. It would be years before I realized how right he was.

Before Coach Magee showed up at our school, we did our own thing. I was playing high school baseball in the seventh grade and was the ace pitcher for the team. It seemed every time we played a game I was the starter pitcher. I didn't mind, because I loved baseball and I was big and strong. Little did I know this would ruin my arm by the time I was a senior.

I was also on the high school football team in the seventh grade, but I had no confidence. I would sit on the bench and pray they wouldn't put me in. This all changed after Coach Magee came with Coach Skeeter and Coach Black, whose name belied the fact he was a very large white man. Magee and Skeeter coached us in football and baseball, while Coach Bob Hopkins coached us in football and basketball. I really liked Coach Hopkins, who was also my history teacher. You might say we looked up to him, and one of the reasons was that he was six feet seven inches tall.

I think he had once tried out for the Harlem Globetrotters. I remember him telling us how he had a tooth kicked out when going up for a rebound. He was named the head coach in basketball for Alcorn A & M, the same black college in Mississippi where Dick and I would be offered scholarships in football.

After coaching at Alcorn, he later became the head coach for the Seattle Supersonics in the NBA. I didn't bond with him like I did with Coach Magee, probably because my main sport was football even though I was on the high school basketball team.

I still laugh when I think about the first time we had an away game in baseball against a team not fond of the idea of an all-black team with a bunch of white coaches. Tension was high, and us winning the game only added to it. The next thing we knew, they were cursing and throwing whatever they could find at us. Coach Magee almost wrecked the bus getting us out of there to safety.

Coach Magee encouraged us to work hard in class. I remember how angry he got when the local college, Sam Houston State, refused to offer me a football scholarship because it refused to recruit blacks. He eventually convinced the college to invite me to spring training while I was still in high school.

I was so nervous, thinking about playing against guys already in college and, worse than that, an all-white team. However, Coach Magee convinced me, telling me I was good and that he knew I could do it. Sometimes he would just walk up and put his arm over my shoulder and tell me how proud he was of me.

It didn't take long for the coaches at Sam Houston State to figure out he was right. They finally offered me a full scholarship, which I refused. They then offered it to one of my teammates, Ira Baldwin. However, the following year he was killed in a car accident, after having an incredible year and season.

Coach Magee saw more in me than I saw in myself and pushed and encouraged me more than anyone had before. He gave me confidence in my ability, and it showed when, while still a high school senior, I went to spring football camp with college kids. He thought I was the best and encouraged me to prove it to myself. Even after I accepted a scholarship to Alcorn, which was a powerhouse among black colleges in football, he encouraged me to go to the University of Colorado, a predominantly white university. If I had taken that football scholarship, I would have been the first in our town to earn a scholarship to a major university. To my knowledge, no one, black or white, had done that before.

While I don't negate the influence the other men in my life had on me then, the closest thing to a father figure was Coach Magee. Even though my time with him was limited to a few hours a day for only a few years, it had a profound impact on my life.

He took an interest in my future and me and encouraged me. His discipline was fair and reasonable. He risked ridicule and his own reputation to stand up for me, and he tried to protect us. He was committed to making things better for all of us black kids, even though many of the white folk in town resented him and even despised and ridiculed him for being so kind to us.

Coach Magee and his wife had a young son named Mark who was only about five years old when we met. By the time he was in high school, many of his friends were black. I just saw him and Mrs. Magee last summer, and he told me that even now he is often asked by his white friends why he hangs out with "them coloured boys."

Mrs. Magee told me, "You know, Bruce, things haven't really changed that much around here," referring to the attitudes whites have towards the blacks there.

Coach Magee and his wife, Frankie, also made sure we had lunch, even though her favourite was my best friend, Dick Sowells, who went to the black college I was to attend.

Thanks to Coach Magee, I received several scholarships. Most were from black colleges. I was all set to go to a black college with my best friend, Dick, and join our teammate Rayford Jenkins.

Rayford had blossomed as an all-star middle linebacker. I was expected to start alongside him, as an outside linebacker, while Dick would be the starting defensive back. Dick and I often sat around talking about how awesome it would be for the three of us to play together. However, something happened that would change my mind and my destiny.

One day I was paged to come to the cafeteria. I walked in, and there was a white man waiting to see me. *What did I do wrong?* was my first thought.

He quickly relieved my fear by introducing himself. His name was Chet Franklin, coach from the University of Colorado. Apparently, while recruiting some prospects from a school we played against in Houston, he had seen me play. He told me about the school and informed me that two brothers [biological brothers] from Galveston, Texas, were attending. He asked if I would like playing on national TV before millions of people.

OUR FATHER: THE PRODIGAL SON RETURNS

Man, my eyes became bigger than flying saucers! He offered me a full four-year scholarship with the possibility of starting as a linebacker in my sophomore year. Only one catch existed: I had to take a SAT test and get a certain score.

I smiled and nodded yes, but the thought of having to take the same test as white kids scared me, because we were led to believe they were much smarter. I took the test but figured I couldn't possibly score high enough to get into a major university, especially a white one. I put it out of my mind until Coach Magee asked me how I did. I brushed him off by saying I had decided to go to the black college. The truth is, I was certain I hadn't passed.

About a month before I was to leave for Alcorn State, a letter arrived from the state addressed to me. That envelope sat unopened for weeks. I was sure I had failed, so I wanted to spare myself the embarrassment of having to tell the coach.

Coach Magee wouldn't let up. Every time he saw me he would ask, "What's happening with that Colorado deal?" I finally got the nerve to open the envelope, and to my surprise, I scored high enough.

The final decision whether I would attend college or the university was now mine. I really didn't make up my mind until the last minute. I felt a sense of adventure heading off to this unknown place. It really didn't make much sense to choose Colorado over Alcorn. I would be going there all alone, while going to Alcorn meant being with my best friend, another teammate and one of my coaches.

I remember how surprised and disappointed they all were when I told them I was going to Colorado instead of Alcorn. My mind was made up, and there would be no turning back. I was convinced this was the road to fame and riches.

I have heard it said
You can't judge a book by its cover
I say you can't judge a person by their colour
When I first saw those white coaches
I only saw the colour of their skin
But God saw their hearts
And knew they wanted us to win.
I saw their red faces
And immediately said no
But God saw their hearts
And said yes, so go.

TEN

THE PRODIGAL SON

"Not long after that, the younger son got together all he had, set off for a distant country and there squandered his wealth in wild living" (Luke 15:13 NIV).

I packed the few belongings I had, along with some of Mamma's fried chicken wrapped in tinfoil, and left The Alley for the University of Colorado. It was 1967, and I had just graduated from high school.

The only way I differed from the young man in Jesus' parable The Prodigal Son is that I didn't have any wealth to squander, but I was heading off to an unknown world. I was heading to Boulder, Colorado, and unknowingly for a time of wild living.

My inheritance was a few letters from a girl I was dating in high school, my high school yearbook and a full four-year scholarship to one of the top universities in all of America.

This would be the farthest I had ever been from home and my first time on an airplane. I remember saying goodbye to everyone, including my best friend, Dick Sowells, who was leaving by bus for Alcorn A&M, which was where I was expected to go. I was excited and nervous at the same time.

I remember hearing one of my favourite songs, "Jimmy Mack, when are you coming back," by Martha and the Vandellas, and in my mind I was thinking, *I ain't ever coming back to live in The Alley. When I come back, it's to take Mamma out of here to live in her new home in some far-away beautiful location.*

When I finally arrived in Boulder after flying into Denver, school was still out for the summer. The place was like a ghost town. Not many people were around. What a time to be going to a place like Colorado! This quiet little university town was one of the epicentres for drugs and hard rock in America. In

75

addition, it was a fiery nest of political unrest. There were demonstrations for everything, including the Vietnam War. Angry student protestors would often burn the American flag and draft cards in the streets.

The women's lib movement was also in full swing. Women burned everything from bras to panties, demanding equal rights in the boardrooms and bedrooms and access to abortion clinics. Women wanted to have the right to have as much sex as the men. On top of that were civil rights demonstrations for blacks.

The University of Colorado was a haven for social activists and self-interest groups. It wouldn't be long before I started my own group, called "it's all about me," recruiting my set of groupies.

It was a lot to deal with all at once, especially for a black kid with no real father, leaving home for the first time. It would have been nice to have had a father to help me deal with so many unexpected changes, but I had to figure these things out on my own. They didn't even have black coaches at the University of Colorado when I first arrived.

They arranged summer jobs for the new recruits and put us up in a dormitory on campus. I found out later the type of summer job they gave you was determined by their expectations of you as a recruit. They got me a job in a brickyard, because I guess they figured I was built like a "brick outhouse," and arranged for me to ride to work with a white kid named Jim who was from Boulder.

I thought it was ironic that the first kid I got to spend time with had the name Jim. When I met him, I felt like asking if his last name was Crow. We never socialized. We rode to and from work together. I don't think we even had lunch together.

I found out there were several "blue chip" recruits who happened to be black, and they stayed in a different place on campus. Their summer jobs were working out and going to summer school.

One of them was Mike, a big offensive lineman from Ohio. Then there was Glen Bailey, the top rookie recruit from Chicago. This guy was supposed to be the anointed one, the saviour, like the running back in the hit movie *Friday Night Lights*. He was expected to lead the Buffaloes to the Promised Land, to the Orange Bowl. He had the look, the swagger and an entourage everywhere he went. Everybody called him Prince Bailey.

There was another rookie named Henry from Louisiana. He was weird. I even thought he might be into voodoo. For no reason this dude hated me. I could never figure out why, because I was only a step above a walk-on. I even thought at any moment I might have been told this was a mistake and they gave the scholarship to the wrong guy.

As a result, I was very reserved. I made sure I was on my best behaviour. I didn't want them to send me back to The Alley. I was like a prisoner out on parole. Every day I went to work and then back to my room.

The idea that maybe someone made a mistake and that if I messed up I would be sent home constantly haunted me. It would take almost four years before I realized I really belonged there. I was haunted by a fear of rejection.

I spent a lot of time reading the letters from my girlfriend, wishing I could see her and some of my friends back home. It wasn't long before her letters became fewer and fewer, until she finally stopped writing.

A couple of black guys from Boulder, Colorado, were going to the school. However, the only thing black about these guys was their colour. There was nothing black about their behaviour. They had grown up going to school with white people, and they even sounded white when they spoke. Sonny, one of them, invited me one night to a party. I remember driving in his little MG with the top down, racing up Flagstaff Mountain.

Shortly after arriving, I got the shock of my life. This guy had a white girl-friend. I couldn't believe it. Back home, they would put you behind the walls of the state prison if you stared at a white girl and worse yet death row or death by lynching if they caught you dating one.

I remember in the 1950s when Emmet Till, a young boy from Chicago visiting family in Mississippi, was kidnapped, tortured and murdered for whistling at a white woman. This shocked and horrified many in America, both black and white, and really was one of the sparks of the whole civil rights movement.

After being there a month, I began to venture up to "The Hill." That was the spot where all the action was for kids in university. Tulagees and a place called The Sink were super hot hangouts. I would go there at night to watch the people dance and drink beer. I wouldn't dare ask any of those girls to dance. I felt so out of place.

As summer slowly ended, some of the older players started to show up on campus. Shortly after, school started.

My roommate was one of the brothers from Galveston, Eric Harris, whose older brother, Bill, was the starting tailback. There was Wilma Cook, the starting fullback, Ike Harris, a cornerback, Bill Collins, a defensive tackle, Gene Johnson, an offensive guard, Derrick Faison, a defensive tackle, and Bob Stevens, a 260-pound running back. He and Derrick had transferred from Illinois after a recruiting scandal. Finally, there was Glen and I.

OUR FATHER: THE PRODIGAL SON RETURNS

We stuck out like a few black-eyed peas in a large pot of white rice. This was a totally new experience for most of us. It was 1967, and integration was still a new thing. Many of the schools bringing in black players had a quota on the number they could have at any time. This was the most black football players Colorado had brought in ever. I believe by then all the teams in our conference, "The Big Eight," had at least several "token" black players. However, in other conferences, like the Southwest and Southeast Conferences, which included teams like the University of Texas and the Crimson Tide of Alabama, there was an unwritten policy not to integrate, for fear of the social implications.

I didn't realize they were looking not just for black players who were great athletes but for black players who would fit a certain norm, guys who were well mannered and well-muscled, black guys who would know their place and know whom they should and shouldn't date.

On the one hand there were concerns from the segregationist camp that the black guys would not be satisfied just playing ball with the white guys but would soon turn their voracious appetites for sex toward the white girls. This was fuelled by a combination of fear and stereotyping. While the integrationists had some similar concerns, they could overcome them and prove the naysayers wrong, they thought, if they could find black guys with the right combination of speed and social graces. They were concerned about not just the student population but the alumni and the citizens of Boulder, whom they had to answer to. I felt like the eyes of Texas and Colorado were on me. Even though I was a long way from The Alley, I knew it was a bad idea to step out of line.

We had two terms for two types of blacks. The well-behaved blacks were "house Negroes," while the rebellious ones were referred to as "field Negroes." These were slave terms. The former were dignified, the latter defiant. In simple terms, the field Negro was qualified for the heavy labour and tasks of the field but wasn't refined or trustworthy enough to be let into the master's house.

However, the passion to win forced many of the schools to overlook their racial prejudices and open the doors to more black players. While most of the white coaches dreamed of having such talented players play for them, they dreaded the idea of these players playing with the white co-eds off the field. In fact, we were encouraged to travel to nearby Denver to socialize with our own kind.

I remember the difficulties I faced trying to adjust to being in a predominately white environment. I was a bit hopeful, having had a good experience being coached by white coaches.

This was different. It was one thing to have them as coaches but entirely different to live and socialize with them as your peers. I remember how uncomfortable I was at first being around so many white people, and I'm sure the feeling was mutual. I felt like General Custer in his last stand.

The first time I went to class, I was the only non-white in attendance. I was sitting there waiting for class to start when all of a sudden this great looking white girl came and sat next to me. Man, was I nervous! I didn't dare look at her. I didn't look to the right or the left. I just stared straight ahead or looked down, which is what I was used to doing. What was going through my mind was death row and Jim Crow.

I remember talking to my roommate about that first day in class. He listened and just laughed, especially when I told him about sitting next to the girl from Idaho. He was a sophomore and had figured out the social scene. My roommate was a busy guy on and off the field. I remember there would be a knock on the window of our dorm room at night and he would take off with his pillow and blanket and be gone for hours.

My new surroundings wasn't the only change I had to deal with. I had never been taught little things like how to manage my time or my money. Our family never really talked about this incredible opportunity I had been given, earning a full scholarship to such a great university, or the impact it could have on my siblings or the others who came behind me, people like Dwight and even others who looked up to me like a role model. In many ways, I was representing not just myself but the whole black community.

EL NEGRO

One of the highlights of my freshman year was playing football against the University of Mexico in Mexico City. We were there for almost a week. I had never seen so many people, and it was clear they hadn't seen many black people either. Whenever we would go walking around the city, people would want to rub our skin and feel our hair. I also heard the term *El Negro* for the first time, which I didn't realize then meant "black."

I met this girl who was staying in the same hotel. She was there with her parents, and her father was some high-ranking officer in the Mexican army. We laughed because she spoke very little English and, of course, I spoke no Spanish. We managed with some help from some of the locals working there to arrange a date.

I was down in the lobby waiting for her, and when she finally arrived, she showed up with the whole family—I mean parents, grandparents, sisters and brothers. My teammates laughed so hard as we all stepped out for our walk. We took up the whole sidewalk. I couldn't wait to get out of there. She kept calling me on the phone, but I had my roommate talk to her. She was crying, telling him to tell me she loved me.

"But the way of the wicked is like deep darkness; they do not know what makes them stumble" (Proverbs 4:19 NIV). I didn't socialize much my first year on campus. I went to a few parties in Denver, which was about thirty miles away. The coach actually encouraged this. There was even talk of them providing a bus to get us there and back, but that never happened.

I met a black family from Denver who began to invite me over for weekends. The father would pick me up most of the time. They really made me feel at home. Their son, Ozelle, took me to parties with him. But at the time, I was shy and reserved, like a wallflower that didn't attract any honeybees.

I rarely hung out with any of my teammates, so I didn't get invited to many parties on campus. Glen and Big Bob were roommates, and they began to invite me to some parties. I remember going to several where Big Bob got drunk and began to cry. We soon discovered that when this happened someone was about to experience the wrath of a 260-pound runaway train. This was a scary thing to witness, and no one wanted to get in his way.

One night we were at a party and Bob got drunk. Again he started to cry, only this time, and for no apparent reason, Glen and I were the targets of his wrath. We huddled in the bathroom, trying to figure out what we would do.

Our first thought was to run, but we decided that together we might be able to overcome him. So we confronted him, and instead of trying to hurt us he began to cry and hug us, telling us we were his little brothers. Unfortunately, some other innocent bystander became his next victim.

I remember another night Bob got drunk in the dorm and began to cry. He stormed down the hall and kicked in the door of a room with two white kids. You should have seen the look of terror on those guys' faces.

Fortunately for them, Glen, Derrick and I were there to calm him down, but not before he punched Derrick in the eye. We ended up ordering pizza and sat laughing and eating until early morning.

In my freshman year, Glen and Bob began dating two roommates who lived off campus. Before long, they began to have parties at their house. These girls were white and had two other roommates.

This was the highlight of the week, going to one of their parties. Many of the black players on the team were there, along with some of the local girls and guys who lived in Boulder. After a while I became comfortable enough to ask one of the girls who lived there for a dance.

Well, it wasn't long before I became involved with one of the roommates, and before you knew it Glen, Bob and I would often bump into each other leaving the next morning for class.

Not long after, I became involved with another roommate, who moved out and got her own place. This was the beginning of sowing my oats, and before you knew it I was like a wild horse surrounded by mares.

By the end of my freshman year, I had adjusted to life as a university athlete. Going to a major university as an athlete was an amazing experience. We had everything, including special training tables where they served three meals a day. It was like a five star resort. We had the best of the best and could go back as many times as we wanted at every meal. Our favourite was the steak. We would often wrap up a few for a midnight snack. We also had study hall with tutors to help us with our homework.

My first summer and fall was like being a young rooster in a henhouse, and my first spring would be my coming-out party. I couldn't imagine there was any place on earth like Colorado in the spring. The leaves on the trees would begin to appear, and soon after things would start to blossom, and I don't mean just the trees.

Many of the students would go to Mexico or somewhere warm for spring break. They would change from their winter covering to their spring attire, and you knew spring had sprung. One of the best places to check out the spring collection was around the fountain just outside the student union building. There would be people lying out enjoying the sun, people playing music, lots of chatter and laughter and loads of bikinis.

This was also the time when the parties and picnics started at Flagstaff Mountain. It was like a big fairy-tale you never wanted to end. Several of my friends and I often crashed one of the many parties pretending to be hippies. This was the Jimmy Hendrix, Janis Joplin and Bob Dylan era, and their music was playing 24/7. It was the perfect music for that time.

It was a cool period in America when students promoted peace and got high. Everything was free and easy with lots of drugs and liberal lovemaking everywhere. Our drug of choice was sex.

On the other hand, it was a tense time with growing antiwar and civil rights demonstrations. These messages were central to Dylan's music.

OUR FATHER: THE PRODIGAL SON RETURNS

Playing football was like a reality check. Once football practice started you were quickly reminded why you were there. When we started spring practice, freshmen had a chance to compete for the varsity team. I had a decent freshman year but nothing outstanding. We only played about four games. It was time to show my game and stake my claim as the starting linebacker.

I had impressive practices and became an early favourite to start after demolishing a bunch of guys in the pit. The setup area was about four feet wide by five feet deep. The defensive player's job was to shed a blocker and tackle the runner. Like in The Alley, there was only one way out and on the field. It was either around or through the defender.

This drill separated the cream from the milk. I quickly earned respect for my tenacity in the pit. I was like a guard dog in a junkyard, and nobody got past me on or off the field.

By the time my first school year ended, I had adjusted to university life and was looking forward to a successful sophomore year on and off the field. The school year ended shortly after spring training, and I was off to Chicago for the summer to work in construction for a man whose son was on the team.

I left knowing I would be a starting linebacker as a sophomore when I returned. I also left thinking I had at last crossed the Mason Dixon line and I had finally escaped Jim Crow and death row.

I left my freshman year feeling I was actually equal to the white players, which gave me a sense of entitlement. Not only could we shop in the same candy store, I didn't just have to look and drool. I could now touch and sample the candy, and there was lots to sample.

Little did I know that although I could play football with them like I had played with Butch as a kid, like then there were certain things I was not entitled to.

We stood out like black-eyed peas
In a large pot of rice
Like a scientific experiment
And we were the lab mice.

ELEVEN

BLOWIN' INTO THE WINDY CITY

"The wind blows where it wishes, and you hear the sound of it, but cannot tell where it comes from and where it goes. So is everyone who is born of the Spirit" (John 3:8 NKJV).

The extent of my knowledge of Chicago came from a famous song by Lou Rawls depicting the cold winds of Chicago. My first experience of "the windy city" was dangling hundreds of feet from a high-rise overlooking its skyline.

Dr. Phil, became famous years later in the city of Oprah, says there is part of the human brain that doesn't develop until we get into our twenties. That partially explains why I hung outside the tallest granite building in the world, at times without a safety belt.

I spent the entire summer working construction in Chicago and would earn the most money I had ever seen. Glen arranged for me to stay with his parents, who lived on the Southside. What this meant was getting up early to take a forty-five-minute bus ride to the famous L train so I could get downtown by seven o'clock in the morning to start work.

Glen's mother, Mrs. Bailey, made me feel right at home. On the other hand, I didn't get the same feeling from his stepdad, Big John Bailey. Something about him made me feel uncomfortable, so I just kept my distance when he was around.

I had worked in construction before, but nothing prepared me for this. It was manual labour and very dangerous. A number of workers died that summer from accidents.

It took me a while to get used to this kind of work, but before long I was hanging outside fifty, sometimes sixty, storeys high. You would think I was King Kong.

Glen had come there with me when school was first out, but he had to go back to Colorado for the summer. Before he went back he introduced me to a few friends so I would have people to hang out with for the summer.

It was fun going down to the beach on the lakeshore on a hot summer night. There was always lots of activity, people playing conga drums and singing and a lot of very talented people just hanging out, having a good time. The night would often end with us stopping at Lims for some of their famous barbeque.

The highlight for me that summer was when Mohammad Ali came into Lims and sat down next to me while I was having lunch. I tried to act cool, but I was freaking out. This was the summer of 1968. He had been stripped of his title for refusing to fight in the Vietnam War, but for me and many other black people he was still the champ. I did manage to say a few words to him and got his autograph. He had been using his new name for a while, and when someone addressed him as Cassius Clay he would politely smile and recite his new name.

I will never forget my last day at work. Just minutes before I walked out to leave, an iron slab fell from above us and absolutely flattened a car. It looked like a mangled pancake. I think it finally sunk in that day how close I had come to death on many occasions. I left Chicago and went home to Texas a couple of weeks before school started.

Little did I know then that I would end up living in Chicago. It was 1971, just after I left university. I would discover the wind wasn't the only cold thing you had to deal with in that city. I encountered the type of racism in Chicago I thought only existed in the South. Actually, it hit me harder there, because it was unexpected. While Chicago was not legally segregated, it sure enough was separated. The spirit of Jim Crow had made its way to Chicago, and from the club scene on Rush Street to the mean streets of Cicero, I would experience the painful reality.

After I left a club one night with a girlfriend, we were pulled over by the police. Glen was in town to visit his daughter, and he let us borrow his car. He apparently had put in too much transmission fluid, and it was smoking.

The problem wasn't that we were stopped but where we were stopped. This was without a doubt the worst place in Chicago you could be stranded as a black man. We were told not to move the car, and often they would circle to make sure we were still there. I didn't want to risk being arrested for moving the car, so I decided to phone Glen. I told my girlfriend to stay in the car and lock the door.

I walked a bit looking for a phone. I noticed one just inside the front door of a bar. It was getting late, so I went inside to make the call. The minute I stepped inside, I felt like a character in a typical old western movie where the stranger walks in, the music stops, and all eyes are on him. All eyes were on me, and if looks could kill, I was a dead man. I rang Glen, but there was no answer.

Before I could try again, one of the guys got up and walked over to me. "Boy, you ain't welcome in here," he said.

Before long, a couple more guys joined him. They started to threaten me, calling me nigger. To make matters worse, my girlfriend had gotten out of the car. When they saw her, they went crazy.

I shouted, "Get back in the car and lock the door!" They came closer, but I didn't move. I don't know who was more afraid, them or me. I was in very good shape, and my tight shirt showed off my massive arms, which it seemed made them reluctant to jump me.

Suddenly one of them disappeared behind the building. I figured he was either going for more help or to get a gun. I noticed the police circling again, but they didn't stop. I'm convinced they knew if I stayed there long enough I would be seriously hurt. As soon as they went around the corner, I jumped in the car and took off.

There was so much smoke coming from the engine it looked like it was on fire. I didn't care. I wasn't going to stop until I got where we were going.

Another divine intervention, I think. While Chicago is still called the windy city, I'd say now it's a warmer city since the arrival of Oprah and Michael Jordan.

I saved up eleven hundred dollars that summer in Chicago. I felt I was rich, but there's an old saying, "A fool and his money will soon part ways." Well, I parted with mine in one shot.

I had my heart set on buying my first car. After some searching, I spotted an ad in the Houston paper for a standard five-speed 1964 black GTO, with three carburetors. I test-drove that thing all the way home and thought I was the coolest dude in all of Texas.

My friend Dick was also home for the summer, so we spent time hanging out and riding around in my hot wheels. I felt like a million dollars when we went to the local restaurant and waited for the waiter to come over and take our order.

We were a real hit with the girls that summer. We hooked up with a couple of girls who before we went to college wouldn't have known we were alive. Now they were giving us the time of our lives.

OUR FATHER: THE PRODIGAL SON RETURNS

This was going to be my year, my time to shine. It was the fall of 1968. My summer in construction had helped me get ready to stake my claim as the starting linebacker. Having my own car would only add to my "cred."

I was flying high as I left The Alley on my way back for my second year. I could hardly wait to show off my new ride to my teammates. Many of our white teammates had cars, but for the brothers this was a big deal.

I had spent most of my hard-earned money buying the car, and it never dawned on me that my $15-a-month allowance as an athlete wasn't even enough to buy gas, let alone pay for any car repairs. Neither did I think the car may be a lemon.

Well, before I arrived back at school, the clutch blew out.

I managed to keep it on the road with some help from friends who would pitch in to buy gas and oil. Several times I had to hit up Uncle Beji or Daddy Walter for a loan when I needed some serious repairs.

By this time I was beginning to change, and before my sophomore year ended I was close to the edge. Dr. Jekyll would soon become Mr. Hyde and bring terror to many students and citizens of Boulder.

Going into our sophomore year, I was ready and eager to step up to varsity and start. By the time we played our first game, I was the starting linebacker.

Being a university football player was a big deal. It meant getting invited to parties. I couldn't understand how the white players could drink so much beer. We had one thing on our minds, and it wasn't getting drunk.

Keg parties were the big thing then on campus. I witnessed some super gross behaviour when my white teammates got drunk. The girls also were wild when they had too much to drink.

It was clear to me then that the white guys on the team were wired differently from us black guys. However, I realize now it wasn't just that; we had different interests.

Most of the black guys there either were from single-parent homes or had unhealthy relationships with their fathers. Our behaviour reflected that unfortunate reality. I say this because I realize now that some of my white friends who had no fathers or an unhealthy relationship with their fathers displayed many of the same behaviours. Like us, they were angry and aggressive. Getting high on drugs or alcohol and being sexual promiscuous are also symptomatic behaviours of many boys and girls, white or black, who grow up either without a father or with one who is abusive or neglectful.

My problem was that as a "fatherless" kid I embraced the rebellious behaviours and being the "bad boy," missing practice, getting into trouble and threatening the "status quo" that my coaches, who were my authority figures, had set up. So they dealt with us by making an example of me.

My journey to the dark side began shortly after I was benched and would continue for almost two years before I was even aware I was lost.

I was gradually moving deeper and deeper into the darkness. My rebelling included everything from skipping class and missing training to bullying many of the students and picking fights with strangers. I used girls to get what I wanted. I sold drugs, carried guns, stole and ripped off all kinds of people.

I became the go-to guy on campus. People would come to me for advice, protection and favours. I became a role model for many of the younger players, as well as other students, black and white. I was the ringleader. Many people followed me.

This was a problem, and like in days gone by, white folks would have to make an example of me to keep the other guys in line. I was upgraded from just having a bad attitude to being a bad nigger, which is what they called blacks who wouldn't conform to their expected norm or suffer in silence. The problem was, many so-called bad niggers were the ones who had the charisma to lead and influence others into rebellion.

The best way to have the good blacks toe the line was to either break the bad ones like a wild horse or make an example out of them of what not to do if one wanted to succeed as a collegiate or professional athlete.

Glen took a different approach to his disappointment. He was more diplomatic. They would give him the job of entertaining high school players they were trying to recruit. In addition, he would often come to me to recruit the girls. He had instructions to keep them away from me because I would tell them how things really were.

We were like raging bulls
In a china shop
And felt there was no way
We could be stopped.
We felt invincible
But really were fools.
Because in the game of life
God rules.

TWELVE

OUTRUNNING THE TEXAS TORNADO

"They sow the wind, And reap the whirlwind"
(Hosea 8:7 NKJV).

After a year I had adjusted to the reality that I was out of The Alley physically. But the baggage of my past, not really knowing my father or having the kind of stable background I had craved, haunted me, like a Texas tornado making its way west across the plains to Colorado's Rocky Mountains. Like a twister on a rampage, it left a path of destruction; everything in its way was swallowed up and destroyed.

My tornado included not only my experiences with my father and stepfather, The Alley and all that represented, but also the larger specter that faced all black people in America at the time: Jim Crow, the minstrel shows, segregation and discrimination.

I had seen the walls of Huntsville State Prison where people waited for their date with Old Sparky and realized that for many of us our lives were overshadowed by a sense of impending doom, just like that prairie twister.

But even more than my external circumstances, which on the surface had infinitely improved, the storm—the sense of anger, aggression and entitlement—was bubbling up inside of me, out of control. It seemed there was no way to suppress it or control it, and my experiences at Colorado only made it worse.

I had gone from an anonymous, disenfranchised black kid living in The Alley in Huntsville to an athlete attending an upscale white university on a football scholarship, with an opportunity to play on national television in front of millions.

But while I was allowed in the candy store, my black teammates and I were not permitted to sample the candy; that was clear, and our youthful ignorance and, worse, our defiance over this was about to derail the whole venture.

OUR FATHER: THE PRODIGAL SON RETURNS

The situation reminded me of *The Wizard of Oz*, where Dorothy gets sucked up by a big Kansas tornado and ends up in the Land of Oz. Here I was in a strange land, thinking I had left The Alley and much of what it represented, only to end up in the Land of Odd. It never dawned on me that I would have to deal with another kind of Jim Crow, except in this case it wasn't Ol' Man Reiner from Huntsville or Daddy Rice in blackface; it was the head coach, named Eddie Crowder. He didn't come out and call me a nigger like Ol' Man Reiner had done to my stepfather or wear a black face like Daddy Rice, but he carried the same racist attitudes towards blacks. It was hidden until interracial dating exposed him. While it was all right to have blacks on your team to win, in the hearts of many we were still considered monkeys and not men.

THE WILD BUNCH

In the summer of my sophomore year, I met three guys who played football. Two of them were from other schools and hoping to transfer to CU. The third had just finished high school and was one of the top college prospects in the whole state. He was the one Colorado wanted to sign.

We started to hang out together, and so began the days of "the wild bunch." We adopted that name after watching the movie of the same name starring Ernest Borgnine, Warren Oates and William Holden. It was one of the first movies to use special effects. It really had an impact on us, and after watching it about a dozen times we were ready to act it out live on the CU campus.

We started wearing long duster coats and gloves with the fingers cut out. We copied the style from another movie, and to be authentic we began carrying guns. I carried a .38 automatic, and we had a couple of 12-gauge shotguns.

A guy we called Snakeman was the main instigator. His real name was Mark Morris, a brown-skinned brother from Denver and apparently from a good home, although he claimed he had no parents. Snakeman was smart and spoke perfect English. He reminded me of someone who should have been on the dean's list.

I honestly believe looking back that he pretended to be bad to be accepted, to fit in. He was also funny and would keep us in stitches as he imitated people. The most hilarious was his impersonation of one of the white coaches.

He was slick, and that's why his nickname was so appropriate. He was a smooth operator. Often he would pick us up driving a fancy car. He would go to a local car dealer and pretend to be a star football player on the verge of going pro. Unbelievably, they would let him leave his wreck of a car and drive off with a new demo and often keep the car for up to a week

OUTRUNNING THE TEXAS TORNADO

I remember one time he answered an ad in the paper to drive a convertible Jaguar to California. It was spring break, and he asked me to go with him. We drove that car in L.A. about ten days before bumping into the owner at a popular restaurant.

Then there was Chuck from Denver. We called him The Black, a name we picked up from one of Clint Eastwood's movies. Chuck's skin was virtually blue-black. He was a mean dude but an amazing athlete. Not only was he a great football player, he excelled in basketball.

Then Dotson joined the bunch. A scary looking kid from Denver, he had been banned from his hometown for getting into trouble. However, because he was a star football player he was sent to a remote town in Colorado. He had no parents and apparently had been given his own place to live in, along with living expense money, while he went to school to play football. He was one of the top high school prospects in Colorado State.

Dotson was a big kid who just wanted to belong. However, he was dangerous. Many times we got phone calls from people he terrorized, and often they were girls.

Chuck and Dotson liked to get high, especially on pills. I remember that summer they tried LSD, a favourite for many of the musicians and students at that time. The Snakeman and I never got high, even though most people thought we were because we behaved like a bunch of crazy people.

They were the perfect trio for me. We were angry at the world, especially the white coaches, and we wanted revenge for the bad things that happened to us. I realize now we were carrying a lot of childhood baggage and unresolved issues. We were walking time bombs ready to explode.

We felt we were justified in what we were doing and that the world owed us something. We were determined to get it, even though it meant hurting people. Trying to justify wrong behaviour is a sign of a hardened heart, which leads to a seared conscience.

A new club called the Skunk Creek Inn became our hangout. Al, the owner, was a small Jewish man who got nervous if someone sneezed, so you can imagine what he would be like when he saw us coming. He would run his hand over his face, probably hoping we would disappear.

Al, however, was a very good businessman. We didn't have a problem with him, and when we first started going there, we hadn't done anything serious yet. We beat up a few people, but that was outside in the parking lot, usually after the club closed.

OUR FATHER: THE PRODIGAL SON RETURNS

We would go in and position ourselves at our station, waiting for the signal to strike. I would stand around wearing my dark glasses and a mean look on my face.

Often in other clubs, while people were dancing and having a good time, one of the guys would go right in the middle of the dance floor and pick a fight. Before you knew it the place would empty out, just like in a John Wayne movie. Once we physically removed a couple from the dance floor at Skunk Creek Inn and took them outside for some roughing up.

Another night several of my white teammates, one of them a running back from Denver, showed up at the club with a couple of linebackers. By this time, I had quite the reputation. The running back from Denver, who was a year ahead of me, decided he would put me in my place. He walked over and without blinking took my sunglasses off my face. I jumped on top of him, and in seconds we were butting heads like two wild bulls. I overpowered him quickly, and while I was hammering his head with my fist, several guys intervened to break us up. I left him with a black eye, adding more to my rep as a guy no one should mess with.

We spent the whole summer stealing, crashing parties and selling drugs. We actually crashed a party that summer pretending to be on the prowl for some pills and ended up instead holding the people at gunpoint and ripping them off of all their stuff.

I sold drugs to have money to buy clothes and other things I wanted but couldn't afford. I walked around campus carrying lids of weed in my pocket. I once kept as much as several kilos under my bed in the dorm. Hippies would front us the stuff, and we would sell it and take our cut. How I survived those dark days, I don't know.

Our front man was this little white guy from Boulder who became our side-kick. He was a nobody until he began to hang with us. He loved the respect and the attention he got from hanging out with university football players.

We had a number of complaints from the university police, but we never paid much attention to them. They often bent the rules for athletes.

However, that summer the Boulder police charged us for beating up a bunch of white students. When the cops came knocking, I was carrying a .38 pistol. I hurriedly hid it under the stairwell. When I went back for it, to my surprise it wasn't there. I shake my head in disbelief when I think how insane I was.

Our day in court finally came, and the unthinkable happened. One of the guys we beat up was in the middle of his testimony when the judge ordered a recess and took all of us into a private chamber. The guy giving his testimony began to speak, but the judge told him to shut up. After a few minutes, he ordered all of our accusers to wait outside. He asked us to tell our side of the story.

He listened and then told us there were a lot of Ku Klux Klan members in Colorado and that some of them were very influential supporters of CU. We didn't know whether to believe him or not, but he was very convincing.

After talking with us, he let us go with not so much as a fine or probation. We figured this guy was either nuts or really concerned for our well-being, so we decided to cool it for a while.

YOU REAP WHAT YOU SOW

Later that summer one of our friends had a house party. I attended alone because my three amigos were off doing something else. We were dancing and having a good time when a bunch of Chicanos walked in and crashed the party. Shortly after arriving, they tried to force the girls to dance with them.

The party's host asked if I would suggest to them that they leave, and of course, with my reputation, how could I say no? I went over to the leader and tried to talk him into saying adios.

I made the mistake of inviting him outside, figuring the other guys I knew would back me up. Once outside, I noticed I was alone with a whole lot of angry Chicanos. Guys carrying knives, chains and tire irons surrounded me.

I had two choices, fight or flee. I decided to run. I wasn't carrying a gun, but if I had been, I'm sure I would have used it, because I feared for my life. I managed to duck behind an apartment complex. As I looked out quickly to assess the situation, I noticed only three or four of them following me. I decided I'd take a stand.

The leader pulled a knife, and as the gang closed in, they began taunting me like a cornered animal.

I looked down and noticed some large rocks. I picked one up and smashed the guy holding the knife in the face. He went down, and I didn't stick around to assess the damage.

A friend of mine lived nearby, and so I decided to head to her place for cover. My heart was beating loudly in my chest. I thought for sure it was over for me, that my days at CU would end and I would be going to jail. My mind was running like a rabid dog as I kept thinking that my past transgressions had caught up to me and I was going to have to pay.

I called home and spoke to my older sister, Peggy, who managed to calm me down.

My friends finally showed. All were ready to take revenge. They went back to the party, beat up a couple of guys who refused to help and roughed up the girl who had the party before walking out. This was a summer of insanity, and I was glad it was ending. None of the three guys managed to get into CU, and I'm glad for them and for me that they didn't.

I managed to do just enough work to stay in school, but not much had changed regarding my status as a player. The closest I got to playing was during practice every week. I felt lost, with no hope of ever being discovered by pro scouts.

The last time I saw Mark the Snakeman he was married and settled down with a beautiful wife and children. They told me Dotson was killed after serving time in prison.

Chuck, whom we called the Black, went on to have a successful career as a college football coach at Boise State. After college he apparently joined a motorcycle gang, was injured in a motorcycle accident and was permanently paralyzed from the neck down.

"War, what is it good for? Absolutely nothin'!"
Lyrics from the Edwin Starr Motown hit "War"

There was a war raging inside me. What had started as a small storm back in The Alley was now that major tornado gathering momentum and destroying everything in its way.

I decided that since I wasn't going to play, I would take my anger out on my teammates. I geared up and taped up for practice as if going into battle.

On one particular day, I was out for blood and decided to terrorize our starting unit. The starting running backs were Bobby Anderson and a guy named Ward Walsh. It was the fullback's job to block the linebacker, and no one could get the job done. They tried one after another to block me.

Finally, out of frustration and concern for their golden boy Bobby Anderson (who ended up in the College Football Hall of Fame), they decided I should be the one to block for him. So I changed over to offence and blocked for Bobby, loving the challenge and wiping out anyone who got in my way.

After practice, I was told I would be switched to offence. I knew exactly what they were doing. It was a message telling the other black players who the straw boss really was. I knew they were hoping I would just give up and quit, but I was determined to play on that team before my time there was up.

I shed my large lineman shoulder pads for smaller ones and changed my number from 61 to 32, the number of my idol Jim Brown. Little did they know that this was my dream, to have a chance to finally play offence.

I took to my new position as a fullback like an eagle to flight. I was the fourth or fifth fullback on the depth chart but quickly worked my way to number two.

It was apparent to everyone I should have been starting, but the coaches were determined that I wasn't going to play. Even though I didn't get to play in a game, I got a chance every week to show what I could do. My speed and agility made me a natural fullback, and my strength made me like a runaway train. As I ran the ball in practice, would-be tacklers would bounce off me or end up being taken for a ride as if on the back of a bus.

My first real action came against Kansas. The team had future all-pro John Riggins at running back and Bobby Douglas at quarterback. Douglas would go on to star for the Chicago Bears. They also had an All American middle line-backer named Emery Hicks. This guy was like the Tasmanian devil. He was extremely fast and a punishing tackler.

The starting fullback, Ward Walsh, and I were roommates on the road. Before we went to bed, the topic of our conversation would always turn to Hicks. It was a dogfight, and Hicks was in on most of the plays.

Walsh pulled up lame, but they put someone else in before me. A close game, it was in the third and about four yards deep in our territory, with not much time left.

They sent me in to block for Bobby, but the quarterback called an audible because they knew Bobby would get the ball. It was fullback off tackle. He handed me the ball, and off I went. Forty-five yards the first time I touched the ball.

There was another crucial down where we needed to get three yards to keep possession, and they called my number again. I was hit at the line but managed to break the tackle for a four-yard gain. My teammates were going crazy. Mike Montler, our all-star offensive tackle, patted me on the back and said, "Good job, kid." I didn't play much after that, but I was content just waiting for another chance.

We were later invited to play in the Liberty Bowl in Memphis against Bear Bryant's Alabama Crimson Tide. By then I was very confident as a running back and was dying to show the world what I could do. My friend Glenn Bailey and I decided we would take a little trip to New Orleans because we wanted to visit a friend of ours who had transferred from Colorado to Tulane.

OUR FATHER: THE PRODIGAL SON RETURNS

We left right after practice because we had a midnight curfew. New Orleans was close to four hundred miles, and though it would be tight, we were sure we could make it there and back in time. We were probably going a little past the speed limit, but we weren't tearing up the highway.

About 150 miles from New Orleans, highway patrol officers pulled us over for speeding. Two mean looking white cops with southern drawls drove up beside us and said, "Follow us."

We drove for what seemed like an eternity in the dark night along narrow and rugged back roads. I could hear my heart pumping. Glen kept looking to see if anyone might be coming behind us. I began to think of those stories I had heard of blacks disappearing in swamps along this stretch, many turning into food for the alligators.

Glen was driving, and on several occasions we thought of trying to make a run for it, but we were lost and didn't know how to get back to the main highway. We finally stopped in the middle of nowhere at this huge jailhouse.

I had a pistol in the glove box and was debating whether we should take the gun with us just in case. I remember how big the cops were, real bubbas, with thick tobacco-chewin' southern accents. We expected those ol' boys to change into their white Casper the ghost KKK gowns at any moment.

"What's your name, boy?" drawled one of them. The hair on my neck stood up.

I was so mad I was about to explode. Glen was cool and quickly told him his name. He asked me again, "What's your name, boy?" Then he made the comment. "Y'all are a big un!"

My teeth were clenched and my jaws tight. I said, "Bruce." We told them we were football players down to play a bowl game.

They fined us one hundred and fifty dollars, all the money we had to get us to New Orleans and back to Memphis. I am convinced that what saved us from the swamps was the fact we were football players.

We finally made it to New Orleans and went immediately to find our friend on the Tulane campus. She gave us some money for gas, and we headed back that night. We showed up the next morning just before practice was over. At least we had a good seat to watch the game from the bench while listening to the racial insults yelled at the black players. There were reports of several guys being spat upon.

At least we won the game. Even though I was disappointed I didn't get to play, it felt good that our team kicked their behinds.

OUTRUNNING THE TEXAS TORNADO

Although I had stopped carrying guns and selling drugs, I was still skipping class and hanging out at clubs every night. Time was flying away, and I wasn't going anywhere.

My junior year started out pretty much the same. With the wild bunch disbanded, most of the action was limited to partying and selling drugs occasionally. I discovered I didn't need to do that because there were plenty of girls who were willing to spend their money to get us the things we wanted.

I had no shame in taking their money. In fact, I felt I was only getting back what was taken from me. It's amazing how we justify doing wrong. Mamma would have killed me if she knew what I was doing.

The coaches could have solved a lot of the problems with the black players by just bringing in our mothers. On the other hand, like a lot of single moms today they probably would not have believed that their babies were capable of such terrible things.

The partying continued, and we had a new crop of girls who loved to party. They had house parties that would go all night. We were like junkies; our drug was sex, and instead of sharing needles we shared many of the same girls. James Brown's "Say It Loud—I'm Black and I'm Proud," Sly and the Family Stone's "I Want to Take You Higher" and Earth, Wind and Fire set the mood for many all-night parties, leaving little time for training or studying.

I later turned things around toward the end of my junior year when, as I know now, God intervened.

I was strutting my stuff and talking loud
Singing Brown's Sex Machine
Or I'm Black and I'm Proud
But my pride was a mask
And my strut was too
Because I was lost and scared
And didn't know what else to do
It doesn't matter who you are or who you know
We all eventually will reap what we sow.

"Who would have thought this sweet, little kid in a Roy Rogers shirt would have grown up to be a holy terror?" Bruce wrote. By the way the six guns on his cowboy shirt had more to do with growing up in Texas and all things western rather than as a prelude to the gang symbolism of today.

"The Three Foxes," here's Bruce's mother Dorothy on the right, with her arm around her best friend Margaret (she was the one who fell on the stairs while carrying Bruce's new bike one Christmas in Gainesville, after a little too much Christmas joy), and their other friend Pearline, taken during the 1970s. (*Sadly Dorothy pre deceased Bruce by about a year*)

Daddy Walter, in his later years (he lived to be over 90). He was Bruce's main "father figure" in his early years. "He looked over 9 feet tall to me, and like a ferocious grizzly bear. The rumour that he had killed a man only added to his mystique," Bruce added.

"The Prodigal Son" had arrived in Boulder, at the University of Colorado. However, the opportunity that had been presented to escape the "Alley" and attend a prestigious school on a full scholarship was threatened by disruptive, rebellious behavior, until his "shake up call."

Eddie Crowder (1931-2008) was Bruce's head coach at Colorado. An "Okie" from Oklahoma, the two clashed over Bruce's ability to "toe the line", characterizing him as a "rebel" and "difficult" which were labels that would haunt him throughout his football career.

Having ridden the Underground Railroad to the Promised Land of Canada, Bruce pictured here during his Argo days as a CFL star, recording a "sack" against legendary quarterback Conredge Holloway.

"The End of my Reign", this picture was taken during his last and best season with the Argos in 1979, in which he served as team captain.

From the "Alley" to Forest Hill, the former ball player had transformed himself to Toronto's top real estate salesman. This came as a shock to his former football friends who were surprised that their "moody" team mate displayed an outgoing and dynamic personality and was such a success off the field.

MEMORIAL TRIBUTE
Pastor Bruce Smith

Saturday, January 26th, 2013
11:00am to 12:30pm

Canada Christian College
50 Gervais Drive
Toronto, ON

Tel: 416-391-5000

All are welcome

Hosted by King Bay Chaplaincy
416-366-0818

Sadly, we had to say goodbye to our friend in January of 2013, The Prodigal Son had returned to his heavenly father, leaving us to pick up the mantle of carrying on his work of helping the fatherless.

"A picture is worth a thousand words." During an interview about Bruce after his passing, I was asked "what happened to Bruce that transformed from a growling grizzly bear to a big cuddly bear?" The answer I replied was the transforming power of Jesus Christ. If you don't believe me look at the pictures above and realize that the two contrasting portraits are the same person.

THIRTEEN

THE SIX-INCH CELL

But the Scripture declares that the whole world is a prisoner of sin
(Galatians 3:22 NIV).

One night in my senior year, I woke up at about 5 a.m., which was unusual for me. Normally I would stay up half the night and sleep in, missing most of my classes. That morning I had what I saw as a shake-up call.

I awoke trembling and in a cold sweat. My heart raced along with my mind. I suddenly realized that my life was out of control. Thoughts of going back to The Alley or worse yet to "The Walls" or death row just kept cycling through my head.

For the first time I realized how close I had come to being thrown off the team and put in jail for selling drugs. I had almost killed someone, and on several occasions I could have been killed as I pretended to be this tough gun-carrying super dude.

The six-inch cell, the space between my ears, imprisoned me. However, the difference with my six-inch cell was that I had the key and could actually escape by making the right choices. The truth is, it wasn't Jim Crow, the coach, racism, or fatherlessness keeping me in the six-inch cell; it was my own ignorance and failure to take responsibility for my actions.

I got up and decided to do something I hadn't done for a long time. I went for a run. Like the prodigal son, I had come to my senses. However, unlike the prodigal son, I didn't return to my Heavenly Father or back home to The Alley, but I returned to the team and to classes.

I made up my mind I would work as hard as I could, both on and off the field. This really taught me the power of choice, of making decisions and setting goals. I simply made a decision to go to class and study and to work hard in practice.

OUR FATHER: THE PRODIGAL SON RETURNS

This change of attitude changed my life.

The coach didn't change. Eddie Crowder never changed his mind about interracial dating, proof that it's often our attitudes and responses to other people's attitudes that make the difference.

I wasn't aware of it at the time, but I now know this moment of revelation was a God moment. Even though a change in one's attitude is good, this change is often only superficial and temporary, because real and lasting change starts with the heart. I was still angry and being driven by unmet needs, controlled by hidden faults, the iniquity of my forefathers, so although I made improvements in my attitude and approach to college, much of my behaviour remained unchanged. I realized, however, that I was running out of chances.

I finally got an opportunity to play, with only four games left in my senior year. I know now this opportunity came from the hand of God. I played like a man possessed and found out later I was actually possessed.

That winter they brought in a transfer named John Tarver, who the coaches decided would be the starting fullback. They called me into the office and asked if I would consider redshirting (not competing) for one year, which would provide an extra year of eligibility. They felt with one year to really focus and study the offensive position, I could develop into a big-time running back.

By then, I was fed up with the head games. In spring practice, they had actually tried me at defensive tackle. Once again, I was up for the challenge and quickly learned the position. With my quickness, it was hard for any big ol' slow offensive lineman to block me by himself.

Before the season started, they called me in again and asked me to reconsider redshirting. I said no way. Then they asked what position I would like to try for. I said defensive tackle.

So the season started with me at either fourth or fifth on the depth chart at defensive tackle. I worked hard and went to class. But I still wasn't playing, although I had moved up on the depth chart to number two.

My behaviour was a total surprise to both teammates and the coaches. Not only was I going to class and to practice, I was following all the rules. I began to sow good seeds. Eventually I would reap a good harvest.

There were only four games to go in my senior year, and I hadn't as much as played a down. However, that would change one hot Saturday afternoon while in a game against Nebraska. The guy playing ahead of me, a perennial powerhouse, got hurt. They signalled me to go in.

THE SIX-INCH CELL

We lost the game, but I recorded two-quarter back sacks and was in on a number of tackles. I started the next game against Kansas and ended the season with a breakout game against the Air Force Academy. In those four games, I was probably the best defensive player on the field for our team. In my last regular season game against the Air Force Academy I went berserk. I was in on about 70 percent of all the tackles and had several sacks.

The win against Air Force put us in a position to get invited to another bowl game, and we got invited back to the Liberty Bowl. Many of us didn't want to go back, but after a close vote it was decided that we would accept the invitation. This time we would be playing against Tulane, and my friend who attended Tulane would come to visit me in Memphis.

I also got to be the starting defensive tackle. I played a good game, but this ended my playing days as a Buffalo. It seemed as quickly as it began it ended. It was time to move on, but I really had nowhere to go. There was a very slim chance I might get drafted in the last round. Several people had heard rumours, and that is exactly what they were. My chances were slim and none, and slim had just left town.

There was the war in Vietnam
And the one inside me
Mine had escalated to violence
For the whole town to see
I was on the eve of destruction
And headed for jail
Or even worse
Eternity in hell.

FOURTEEN

THE END OF MY REIGN

Fear the LORD and the king, my son, and do not join with the
rebellious, for those two will send sudden destruction upon them
(Proverbs 24:21–22 NIV).

This was my last year of eligibility, and I knew there was no way I was going to graduate. I was praying there might be a slim chance I may be drafted into the NFL in the last round.

Rumour had it that several pro scouts had inquired about me, but the coaches told them I was bad news because I would lead others astray. They were determined to break me or make an example of me as a deterrent for those who might follow me.

One of my teammates overheard a conversation between a scout and a coach and confirmed this. The same player also told me there were several letters from pro teams addressed to me, but when I inquired about them, I was told they didn't exist.

I think there was no question I had compromised my chances by being "the bad Negro." My coaches had isolated me and restricted my opportunity, not so much because of my football ability or what I did between the lines, but because of what I did and represented outside of them. There are definite lines of authority, and when you cross them, you will be penalized. Respecting authority is one of the most important lessons a father should teach his children.

In many ways, I squandered the opportunity at Colorado—in other words, no graduate degree, no NFL contract. While I had a reason to be angry, they had a right to enforce their authority, and now they were going to use this opportunity to teach those behind me a valuable lesson: if you follow Robert Bruce, the same thing will happen to you.

OUR FATHER: THE PRODIGAL SON RETURNS

I had come a long way from The Alley, but I didn't understand the whole concept of authority and how by challenging it and being defiant about so many things I undermined my chance at success. While I had won many small personal victories, it had been at a tremendous cost to me and my chances to go to the NFL.

Of course, I felt I was right and that the treatment I received was unjustified. While much of it *was* unjustified, that didn't justify *my* behaviour. I believe the core of the head coach's problem was racism and the core of my problem was rebellion and anger.

What I didn't know was, I wasn't only rebelling against the authority of the coaches; I was rebelling against the delegated authority of God, which was a much bigger problem than rebelling against man.

What I didn't comprehend was that, right or wrong, they were the ones in authority and therefore had certain rights. While those in authority may exercise their authority for the wrong reasons, it won't work out well for those who rebel. I soon discovered that my reputation as a rebel would precede me wherever I went.

By the end of my last year of eligibility, they had brought in a slew of black players, including guys like Cliff Branch, who starred with the Oakland Raiders, and J. V. Cain, a tight end who later became a high draft pick in the NFL but died suddenly in his second or third year while playing for the St. Louis Cardinals.

There was Charles Davis, a running back who set many rushing records during his playing days. He later went pro with the Cincinnati Bengals but had his career cut short by a knee injury. There was Larry Brunson, who played for the Kansas City Chiefs and the Denver Broncos. He was one of my best friends, along with Glen, who we called Prince Bailey.

There were several other top prospects there as well, including Bo Matthews, a running back who also went pro, There was also Cullen Bryant, a skinny 175-pound defensive back who overnight transformed into a 240-pound hulk who could run a four-point four-second forty-yard dash.

My nickname was RB, and before long, all the players began to be called by their initials. Everyone wanted to be like RB. There was CD, JV, GB, CB, but there was only one RB. I was somewhat of a legend, and as usual, the legend was more myth than reality. The truth is, I still carried a lot of childhood insecurities, which I hid behind muscles and a face masked with a smile. At least the muscles were not inflated with steroids, as in the case of many would-be collegiate and professional players at that time. I think the fact that I didn't do drugs or even drink alcohol was one of the things people respected about me and in some strange way added to the myth.

I was like a walking paradox, on the one hand friend and protector of the little guy, and on the other hand defiant and tough and very unapproachable. There was danger written all over me, and I never really saw the signs. Yet there were always people who saw something else, a certain vulnerability that girls in particular found attractive. I think it was an instinct to nurture and the challenge of capturing and taming a myth. Looking back, it's hard to even imagine how far away from the light I really was.

The draft came and went, and of course I wasn't drafted. I wasn't surprised, but nevertheless I was disappointed. I was just hanging out, trying to decide what I was going to do. I had a lot of time on my hands, so I occupied myself with partying and hanging out at several clubs.

A guy named Ted Woods lived with his wife, Karen, and young son, Todd, in Boulder. Ted became like a big brother and mentor to me. He was from Philadelphia, had played football at CU and been a member of the track team. He also played football in the Canadian Football League with the Calgary Stampeders in Calgary, Alberta.

Unfortunately, I didn't meet Ted until my last year at CU. He was the mentor I needed. I really admired and respected him. Not only was he a great athlete; he had graduated and was in law school and soon to be a lawyer, which was rare for a black athlete at the time. Ted had a real positive influence on me, and I admired and looked up to him.

Little did I know that the coach at the Air Force Academy had recommended me to a coach in Canada with the Winnipeg Blue Bombers. They had apparently been trying to locate me, but the coaching staff told them I was nowhere to be found.

Going to Canada was the furthest thing from my mind. No kid growing up watching the NFL dreams of going to Canada to play football. For me this was like going to the North Pole. When I thought of Canada, I thought of Eskimos on dogsleds.

By this time, I had a new friend named Chuck, a little Jewish guy from Denver who was into R&B music. He had the largest collection of records I had ever seen. Chuck was into something else too, and it seemed every time we turned our heads Chuck was getting beat up by some football players.

One night at around midnight, I heard someone knocking frantically on my door. When I finally opened it, there was Chuck with a bloody nose and a torn shirt. Four guys he described as big dudes had apparently beaten him up.

We went off to defend our friend. Little did we know these were professional football players.

They were at this place we hung out at called the Catacombs. Chuck went up to one of them, smacked him upside the head, turned and walked away. Seconds after he made it through the door, the guys came out. Snakeman flashed his shotgun. Before anyone could move, I punched one of them in the nose. You could hear the nostril bone crack, but just as his blood started to run down his face, a cop car showed up and ended what could have been a violent if not deadly encounter.

A few weeks later, we were in another fight, this time with a couple of transfer players who were also former marines. Everyone poured outside to watch the action. There were several of them, including this big guy named Jake. He and I went after each other like two angry bison.

I managed to take him down and was trying to punch him but soon realized my hands were full. On top of that, I was out of shape, and by the time he got up, I was gasping for air. I danced around to keep from going down. I was worn out, and so was he. Eventually we shook hands and went home.

The news travelled fast. RB had met his match, and my reign of terror was over.

Chuck, we found out later, had provoked the fight.

Later that year allegations of racism on campus began to surface again, and this time there was an official hearing. It made the headlines, but things quickly settled down. In the meantime, I was still around, just hanging out and enjoying my friends.

When the school year was over, I spent the summer in Chicago. While I was there the Winnipeg Blue Bombers finally located me. They offered me a contract with a thousand dollar bonus. Of course I accepted.

What a difference four years can make! What began as a one-way ticket out of The Alley almost ended in disaster. This can happen to anyone who puts all their hope in their own ability or talent or fails to understand how to respond to life's disappointments.

There are thousands of young people like me who dream of making it big one day as a professional athlete but never realize that dream. In addition, like me many of them waste an incredible opportunity to get a good education that more often than not provides opportunity for a brighter future. This is not to say you shouldn't dream and aspire to be a pro athlete; however, only a small percentage of players are good enough to play at that level. While many like Glen, who definitely had the talent, have their plans to go pro suddenly end with an unexpected injury or some other unforeseen set of circumstances, others like me fail to understand how to respond to those in authority and squander our opportunities out of pride, anger and resentment.

Whether in life or sports there are rules. Some are written; some are not.

Take gravity, for instance. It works the same for everyone regardless of colour. The same thing applies to authority. The best way to deal with those in authority is to submit and not quit, to excel rather than rebel.

We are not responsible for how those in authority treat us, but our response to them is both our choice and our responsibility.

My tenure here was over now
Time for my swan song
But I was clipped like a pigeon
Because I had chosen wrong
I was now the example of what not to do
So learn
Or the same thing will certainly
Happen to you.

FIFTEEN

TRYING TO SOAR LIKE AN EAGLE

They will soar on wings like eagles (Isaiah 40:31 NIV).

I had grown weary trying to figure out what I was going to do. The thought of hanging around the club scene while other teammates were preparing for careers in the pros or in business bothered me. The thought of going back to Huntsville to work in the woods was enough to give me cardiac arrest.

The New York Jets had drafted my best friend, Dick. The Jets had Broadway Joe Namath, but I was like a Broadway show at the end of its run, and it was time to move on.

Coming to Canada was the last chance for me to salvage my football career, but like a lot of Americans who go to Canada, I underestimated the competition and the extent of the reach of my university coach's influence.

I first came to Canada in 1971. It was nothing like I thought it would be. Although I was living in a different country, it was a lot like living in Colorado.

Going to Canada appeared to be the only viable option for me if I wanted to play pro ball. The plan was to go there and get some experience and eventually come back and play in the NFL.

This was a very weird situation. I showed up in Winnipeg on the plane with several other players from the States. I remember the head coach, Jim Spavital, greeting the other players and welcoming them to the Winnipeg Blue Bombers. However, when he got to me, he didn't even shake my hand. "I'll tell you what right now. I hear you are a troublemaker, boy, so watch it!" That was his hello to me.

I didn't know he was an "Okie" from Muskogee who happened to know my coach at CU, Eddie Crowder, who was also from Oklahoma and played quarterback for archrival Oklahoma Sooners.

OUR FATHER: THE PRODIGAL SON RETURNS

I had come a long way north, but Coach Spavital was the ultimate good ol' boy, an Okie who had been a star at Oklahoma State and who for years held the record in the NFL for the longest kick-off return in league history. However, he was cut from the same mould as my head coach in Colorado and obviously, from his comments and demeanour towards me, had been warned by him about me.

I showed up out of shape but managed to have several outstanding practices. The one thing they noticed right away was my quickness off the ball and my strength. On top of that, several of the guys took a real liking to me. One of them was Emery Hicks, the same guy who had been at Kansas. Then there was Mack Herron from Kansas State, a five foot four bowling ball who could fly. Both these guys had been superstars in the Big Eight, the same conference we played in. There was another guy, Dick Smith, who was a starting at one of the receiver positions.

These guys really encouraged me and wanted me to make the team, but I was unhappy there and wanted to leave. Someone had apparently overheard me talking to a veteran player encouraging me to leave and try out in the NFL. After the head coach heard about this, he came to see me.

He said the coaching staff was high on me and I had a good chance of making the team. I had already made up my mind; however, I didn't want to hang around here.

Before the first exhibition game, Dick Smith and I were called into the office and suspended. We walked into what looked like a Klan meeting. It also sounded like one. They accused Dick Smith of influencing me and accused me of being a troublemaker. Suspending us in my mind was the equivalent of tarring and feathering us before throwing us off the team. We were no house niggers, and so we weren't going to get a chance to be in the house.

I was perfectly fine with it, but I felt terrible for Dick, who had only tried to provide some fatherly advice. We decided to go out and see if we could plant some seeds before we left.

We decided to go out on the town before leaving Winnipeg and went downtown to a nightclub. Unbeknownst to us, a group of white guys were not happy we were dancing with the local girls. Before we realized what was happening, we were swarmed by a bunch of guys and had to fight our way out.

These boys intended to put a beating on us. Isn't it funny how what goes around comes around. We were minding our own business and ended up targets, the same thing I had done to so many others back in the Skunk Creek Inn and in other clubs. We reap what we sow, no matter who we are or where we go.

TRYING TO SOAR LIKE AN EAGLE

Training camp in the NFL hadn't started yet, and my friend Ted Woods managed to get me a tryout with the Philadelphia Eagles, because he knew the head coach, Jerry Williams, who coached him in Calgary.

I ended up going to camp with the Philadelphia Eagles in Reading, PA. I had a good camp and made the local papers for several outstanding practices, but I didn't have a whole lot of confidence and I was out of shape and not prepared. I was cut and ended up being sent to a farm team in Hartford, Connecticut.

That didn't last long, because I just wasn't into it, so I left and went back to Chicago, where I spent the rest of the year. Later I played a few games for a semi-pro team in Chicago.

It just so happened that Jerry Williams ended up being the head coach for the Hamilton Tiger Cats in the Canadian Football League the next year. Once again, my friend Ted Woods was instrumental in getting me a tryout.

This time I decided to train, and I got in the best shape I had ever been in. I was a lean, mean and hungry football machine, determined that nothing was going to stop me from making that team. I had a one-way ticket, because I had no intention of returning. My mission was to make that team, and there was no looking back.

I was in a brand new country
With a brand new hope
But I had barely landed
Before they pulled out the rope.
They heard I needed to be kept on a short leash
Because I had the power to mislead the new sheep.
It wasn't long before they called us in.
You Smith boys
Are not what we need to win.

SIXTEEN

RIDING THE UNDERGROUND RAILROAD TO THE PROMISED LAND

One thing I do: Forgetting what is behind and straining toward what is ahead (Philippians 3:13 NIV).

I really didn't know what lay ahead going to Canada, but I knew there was nothing behind me except a possible trip back to The Alley. While going to Canada was not part of my original plan, I know now it was part of God's plan to get me in a position to fulfill His purpose for my life.

I remember coming to Hamilton in the first part of June for training camp. I walked off the airplane wearing a winter coat and a toque in 90-degree weather.

Certainly, after four years in Boulder, playing ball across the U.S. and having spent time working and living in Chicago, I was a lot more worldly than the kid who left The Alley; however, I certainly knew nothing about Canada, except for my brief stay in Winnipeg. I knew nothing of the historical importance of Canada and how a hundred years before I was born the Underground Railroad was a means of escape for thousands of runaway slaves fleeing the tyranny of slavery in the south.

For white European immigrants, America represented the Promised Land, their Israel, but for African blacks, kidnapped and brought across the ocean against their will and thrown into slavery, America was Egypt, a place to escape from to be free. The story is told in the Bible about God sending a man named Moses to deliver the children of Israel from Egypt after they'd been slaves for four hundred years. Like the Israelites, blacks were enslaved in America, for over two hundred years. One of the pioneers of the Underground Railroad was Harriet Tubman, a black woman and former slave to whom they gave the name Moses.

OUR FATHER: THE PRODIGAL SON RETURNS

I had heard of guys going to Canada to escape being drafted into the army. I was going there to hopefully escape the rebellious label that dogged me and the racist attitudes I had encountered so often in my native country. The Canadian League had presented real options for football players who didn't get a shot in the NFL, particularly black ballplayers. In the 1940s there were guys like Herb Trawick, who played for the Montreal Alouettes. Generally, there were more opportunities for black players north of the border, both on and off the field. However, the reality was not quite as idyllic as it appeared.

The concept of bringing black players into the Canadian League was actually inspired by Jackie Robinson breaking the colour barrier in baseball. When Branch Rickey, the Brooklyn Dodger GM, signed Robinson, he first assigned him to their minor league affiliate in Montreal. This way, Rickey thought, he could prepare the world for Robinson's arrival in Brooklyn. He believed Montrealers were more open to blacks, as many famous black jazz musicians immigrated there. Montreal had become a kind of New Orleans north. Even Sammy Davis Junior lived in the city as a young man.

The Montreal Alouettes in the Canadian Football League decided this was a great concept and moved to bring in Trawick. His arrival, however, was not without incident, as a couple of teams in the league threatened to boycott any games involving the Alouettes. When Trawick did play, he received as much racial taunting from the white Canadian players as from the Americans.

Over time, black players were accepted and started to excel north of the border. Guys like Ralph Goldston, Dave Mann, Cookie Gilchrist and Ulysses "crazy legs" Curtis, the first black Toronto Argonaut, became big stars.

In the early 1960s Sandy Stephens from Minnesota starred as a quarterback for Montreal and broke the colour barrier at quarterback. He paved the way for great players like Warren Moon, Chuck Ealey, Conredge Holloway and many others who were not given a chance to play quarterback in the NFL because of their colour.

My career had a less spectacular beginning. I showed up unheralded, but that changed the first day of practice. They set up the pit drill, and I quickly rose up as the pit boss. At one point I was urging them to leave me in the pit until I went through all the running backs and linemen.

The coaches took notice, and I was quickly made an early favourite to start at right defensive tackle alongside CFL and wrestling legend Angelo "King Kong" Mosca from Notre Dame.

We had a great team that year. We had Chuck Ealey, a quarterback from

Toledo who had never lost a game in high school or college, and Tony Gabriel, a future hall of famer. There was John Williams, a vicious corner back from Texas, and Jerome Gantt from South Carolina. We had the fly, Dave Fleming, and the bird, Dennis Shaw. Jerry Sternberg, the only Jewish guy I knew who played football, was with us, as was Garney Henley, who reminded me of Clark Kent off the field and Superman on the field.

Once again, the most unlikely person would have a profound influence on me as a father figure—my white coach, Jerry Williams. I remember going to Montreal to play against the Montreal Alouettes. We arrived the day before the game. At dinner that night, they were serving roast beef, and I requested an end cut. Instead of an end cut, I ended up with a piece of rare roast beef. I was livid, storming out of the restaurant and into my room.

Shortly after, I heard a knock on my door. To my surprise, it was Coach Williams. He wasn't angry and asked if we could talk. He talked a little bit about my past and said he could understand why I carried a chip on my shoulder. Actually, it was a chip the size of shoulder pads.

I was carrying a lot of hostility because of unhealed pain and unresolved issues. I wouldn't discover until years later that this was the main reason for most of my anger and my explosive temper. Coach Williams took an interest in me, telling me I was a very valuable member of the team and part of the Ti-Cat family. For the first time in a while, I felt someone wanted and needed me. We won the Grey Cup in my first year.

Coach Williams was like a father, not just to me but to many others on the team, and I think we won the Grey Cup because we were like a family.

However, I had mixed emotions winning the championship. While many of the players shared their victory with their fathers in the dressing room, I sat on the bench feeling empty. Even winning a championship can't meet some needs.

I enjoyed living and playing football in Hamilton. Being a Ti-Cat in those days was a big deal.

My best friend at the time was a guy named George Wells, who was like a brother to me. Many people thought we *were* brothers. Girls would even mistake one of us for the other.

George was a great athlete, a laid back guy. He was also a professional wrestler. In 1975, he and his former wife, Nancy, moved to Vancouver to wrestle in the off-season. I went for one visit and ended up spending four off-seasons in Vancouver.

OUR FATHER: THE PRODIGAL SON RETURNS

I enjoyed Hamilton. The fans appreciated the players, so we enjoyed lots of favour. I had a good relationship with all the coaches and was particularly fond of Coach Williams.

After my second year in Hamilton, I was traded, not because of the coach but because of a disagreement with management over my contract. I had signed a two-year contract in 1972 with an option. Even though the team didn't make the playoffs my second year, I had another good year. At the time, we played a fourteen-game season. We were informed in the off-season that they were adding two extra games to the regular season. Naturally, we assumed we would be paid for the two extra games. We agreed that if we weren't paid for the extra games, we would refuse to play. I was prepared to stay the course, even if others folded.

Hamilton had a team owner and president who had a reputation for being tough and cheap in negotiations. I had not experienced this side of him. When they first signed me, I was just happy to have a chance to play. The thought of trying to renegotiate my contract after we won the Grey Cup never crossed my mind. However, I felt it was only fair that we got paid for the extra games. I had heard stories of how the owner had intimidated players into signing contracts with little or no increase. This man had a reputation of being a bully and would lock horns with any one.

ONE ON ONE WITH RALPH

Ralph Sazio was a man's man. He was huge, with a fearsome demeanour. He had been a player in the CFL and was someone you didn't mess with or cross. There were rumours that if he couldn't take you out, he had ties to some people who could. In many ways he reminded me of Daddy Walter, and many people, including myself, were afraid of him.

The season was about to start, and this issue still had not been settled. Several players had caved in, but I was determined that if I was not paid I would not play, even if it meant missing the entire season. When I signed my contract it was for a fourteen-game season, and I was still under that contract.

By then, everyone else had decided to play. My refusal meant I was once again branded the rebel.

One early morning, a few days before training camp was about to start, I received a message that Ralph wanted to see me. I arrived in my workout gear, not knowing what to expect.

The meeting started out civilly. Ralph had asked Coach Williams to sit in on the meeting. He finally got to the contract and said, "All the other players have agreed to play except you."

I said, "That's fine; a man has to do what a man has to do, and my mind is made up. Unless I'm paid for the extra two games I won't play."

He then tried to patronize me by saying, "I would like to pay you, but if I did that the others would find out and they would expect to get paid too."

I said, "This is between you and me, and what happens between us is our business."

All of a sudden, he jumped up in a fit of rage, saying, "Who do you think you are? No one wanted you in this league except us."

"That may be true," I said, "but I know there are other teams that would love to have me now."

He was ready to explode. "Smith, you are not that good. As a matter of fact, I can't even trade you, because no one wants you."

He didn't know that I had heard from some reliable sources that several teams were interested in trading for me. So I said, "Oh yeah?" and named off a couple of the teams.

So he said he'd prove me wrong by calling one of the teams. He picked up the phone to call and immediately put it down, saying, "The line is busy."

"Let me try," I said, and that made him even madder.

"Are you calling me a liar?"

"It wouldn't be the first time," I countered.

He looked like a bomb about to explode.

Coach Williams was right in the middle of all of this but didn't say one word. He just kept puffing on his pipe. However, I did notice that his puffs were speeding up.

Unknown to me, Jimmy Simpson, the equipment man, and some of the other players were listening through the door. When I bolted out I almost knocked Jimmy out with the door. I think they were pleased someone had stood up to Ralph. But once again, I would add to my reputation as a rebel.

The next morning George and I were walking down Main Street in Hamilton when several people informed us we had been traded. George was traded to the Saskatchewan Roughriders and I to the Edmonton Eskimos.

I found out later that Ralph, like Daddy Walter, had a kind side. I remember when I saw him after being traded he was very gracious and commended me on how good a player I was.

I spent one year with the Edmonton Eskimos and went to the big game but lost against Montreal. After having had probably my best season to that point, I was traded to Ottawa. I was never really told why, but rumour had it that the coach felt he couldn't control me.

It was clear though to everyone that I was one of the team leaders, if not the leader. The head coach on many occasions singled me out as the example others should follow. Once after losing a game, the coach remarked, "If I had a team full of 61s [referring to me], we would have no problem controlling other teams."

One of my teammates and good friends Larry Watkins chimed in, "That may be true, Coach, but you can't even control the one you have now."

After we lost the Grey Cup to Montreal, we were having dinner, and the coach came over to our table and put his hand on my shoulder, saying, "Number 61 is my main guy; we can look forward to a bright future with guys like him." Whenever I think of that conversation, it reminds me of "Back Stabbers," one of my favourite songs by the O'Jays. He was smiling in my face but would soon stab me in the back.

I assumed he would nominate me as the team's outstanding player or, for sure, defensive player of the year. I was in shock when I wasn't nominated for either. I wasn't the only one shocked. However, this was only the tip of the iceberg.

While I was in Texas a couple of months after the season ended, I got a call from a sports reporter from Canada. He informed me that I had been traded again, this time to the Ottawa Rough Riders. I never heard from the coach. However, when I went back to Edmonton to clear up some business Larry Watkins told me, "Smitty, you know why you were traded. This team isn't big enough for you and Coach Jauch. The man feels threatened by you because he knows he can't control you."

The season in Ottawa was one of the weirdest I had in the CFL. After years of being seemingly invincible, both physically and emotionally, I was derailed by my first serious injury and an unexpected broken heart. I had suddenly lost the two most important things to me. At that time, I took both for granted.

Until that point in my life, I had been in control. Now I had no power to change what was happening, and for the first time since I was a kid, I felt hopeless. I tried my best to change things, but the reality was, I needed changing, and that would not happen for another twenty years.

Ottawa had a great team and one of the most fearsome defenses in the league. They had some real characters, guys like Conredge Holloway, who had been a super All American quarterback at the University of Tennessee; Tom Clements, who preceded Joe Montana at Notre Dame; Wayne Smith and Rudy Sims. Even though I never played once down there because of injuries, I made lots of friends. Said and Nick were Lebanese friends who were in the restaurant business. Then there was Hull, Quebec, with its French culture. We went there six nights a week, dancing and hanging out until early morning. We rarely went home alone.

I remember riding home in a cab one night while the cab driver was listening to the radio. All of a sudden, the sportscaster started talking about me. He said it was a shame the Ottawa fans hadn't seen me play in any games that year, also commenting that I certainly looked fully recovered, the way I was moving on the dance floor across the river in Hull.

Life in Ottawa was great. I had an apartment overlooking the canal. I also got a part-time job working in a local sporting goods store called Ritchie's on Bank Street, not far from the Canadian Parliament Buildings. Herb, the owner, was like a father figure and made me feel at home. Herb is Jewish, and I ended up becoming very good friends with two Jewish girls in Ottawa who often invited me to their home. Their family welcomed me warmly.

Once while I was working at Ritchie's, Margaret Trudeau, the wife of Canadian prime minister Pierre Trudeau, who became notorious for hanging out with the Rolling Stones and in New York's infamous Studio 54, came in and bought something. Another time a crazy girl I met really shook the place up. She was well-endowed and spewing venom because I stood her up, and the guys got a kick out of watching me trying to calm her down.

At the end of the season, I became the property of the Toronto Argonauts after being paid that football season by the Rough Riders. Naturally, they weren't too pleased about that. I certainly was. My goal had been to end up in Toronto because at the time the Argonauts was the highest paying team in the league. I decided to get an agent and enjoy the fruits of being a star player with the highest profile franchise in the CFL.

Well before they knew it
I was back in Canada again
Now I was just the kind of player
This team needed to win
In a few months
I was on the championship team
The lesson for you is
Don't give up on your dream.
Riding the Underground Railroad to the Promised Land.

SEVENTEEN

LADIES AND GENTLEMEN, IN THIS CORNER

For we wrestle not against flesh and blood, but against principalities, against powers, against the rulers of the darkness of this world, against spiritual wickedness in high places (Ephesians 6:12 KJV).

After that weird year in Ottawa, I needed a vacation, so I decided to go to Vancouver for a visit. George had gone there with Nancy and his son, Jason, to wrestle in the off-season. What was supposed to be a two-week vacation turned into a four-year love affair with the city. I stayed in Vancouver the whole off-season and every other off-season until I retired. I found the combination of the mountains, ocean and nightlife irresistible.

Now I was wrestling with the thought of having to go back to Toronto. It had always been a dream of mine as a kid to live in Seattle or Portland. Vancouver was only about a half-hour drive from the Washington state border.

I would go with George to most of his wrestling matches, and by the time I actually started wrestling we had visited practically every town in B.C., many of them only accessible by plane or ferry. It took a while before George finally talked me into giving wrestling a try.

Wrestlers have their own culture, and theirs is a close fraternity. It took a while, but they eventually accepted me as one of their own. In the spring of '76, I began to wrestle on the same circuit as George. He was an amazing wrestler and was on the circuit with some of the greatest and most recognized in the business: Gene Kiniski, who had played in the CFL; Andre the Giant, whose hand was longer than my arm; Jimmy "Superfly" Snuska; Rick "Nature Boy" Flair; Randy "Macho Man" Savage; and my favourite, Big Don Leo Jonathan, who was about six feet eight and three hundred and fifty pounds. They were incredible athletes.

OUR FATHER: THE PRODIGAL SON RETURNS

I had the surprise of my life when I finally got into the ring. It looked easy, but I quickly found out wrestling is rough and extremely dangerous.

Even though this was a different sport, the activities surrounding it were much the same. Like with professional football, there were drugs, booze, and plenty of women trying to score with their favourite wrestler. They even had a name for the women. They called them ring rats, and we were the bait.

That was one of the greatest off-seasons. We travelled throughout the province and into the States. I was even sent to Portland to wrestle on the same card as Hulk Hogan.

On one occasion I was supposed to wrestle an American Indian named Bull Ramos. I remember sitting in the dressing room getting ready for my match. Out of nowhere, this guy comes in and begins mouthing off about how much he hates coloured guys, using the N word. I was about to get up and flatten him when the guys burst out laughing. They had set me up.

The fun times had just begun. During the match, Bull had me in a head-lock. As I turned, trying to get out of his grip, I noticed an old white granny. She was calling Bull Ramos every dirty name I'd ever heard. Screaming at him to let me go, finally she got so upset she reached up with her umbrella and hooked me in the trunks. As she began to try to reel me out of the corner, down came my shorts and out came my big butt for all to see.

Once I got out of the headlock I began to bounce around the ring like a kangaroo, and the fans went crazy. That was the night I earned my ring name "Bouncer Smith."

I wrestled with Andre the Giant
And Don Leo too
They took me under their wing
And showed me what to do
We travelled over the country
George Wells and I
And on many occasions
We nearly died.

EIGHTEEN

THE GOOD SHIP ARGONAUT

He saw the disciples straining at the oars, because the wind was against them (Mark 6:48 NIV).

I arrived in Toronto in 1976 to continue my career as a Toronto Argonaut. Wrestling in off-season had prepared me to stake my claim as one of the best defensive linemen in the league.

The Argonauts had a reputation for being a team of high-priced prima donnas and big-name players from the States, like Joe Thiesmann, Eric "The Flea" Allen, Jim Stillwagon, Noah Jackson and Gene Mack, just to name a few.

This Canadian football team, which derives its name from Greek mythology's Jason and the Argonauts, is one of North America's oldest professional franchises. It started out in the nineteenth century as the Argonaut Rowing Club, which at the time was a rugby club.

Over time, the team, which is from Canada's biggest city, transformed itself, becoming the "Hollywood" franchise of the league. However, it was always trying to bring in American superstars as saviours who could walk on water, only to find out most had feet of clay. The scullers were the ones usually rowing against the wind.

After bouncing around Hamilton and Edmonton and spending a year in purgatory in Ottawa after being injured, I didn't mind the swagger and affluence that came with being a member of "The Boatmen." For me it was a chance to play in Canada's finest city with some of the greatest and best-paid players in the league. Finally it was my chance to be a big-time player in a big-time city and to secure from the CFL big-time pay.

I was now going to be a member of a team I used to love to beat. When I was a Tiger Cat, we hated the Argos because they had the highest paid players. As Ti Cats, we were at the bottom.

OUR FATHER: THE PRODIGAL SON RETURNS

It wasn't uncommon for players on either team to be ejected from a game because of fighting. Both George and I had been thrown out of games. I remember being warned by Coach Williams that if I was ejected for fighting I would be fined, and based on what I was making this would have been very painful.

If we only won two games a year, we wanted it to be against the Argonauts. We had their number. We beat them repeatedly; however, they managed to beat us in one particular game. I lined up against one of their big-name players on the offensive line whom I had fought with because he caused me to be ejected from the game just one week earlier.

Like many of the Argonauts, he was a real trash talker. This guy just wouldn't shut up and wasn't satisfied that they had won. He actually followed me down into the dressing room talking trash.

I never said a word, just got dressed and made my way outside, where the bus was parked to take us back home. However, I had other plans and waited for Noah Jackson, one of the big-name Argo glamour boys, to come out.

He finally came out, and before he knew it, I took him down to the ground and started to punch the lights out of him.

Apparently the newscasters found out about the fight and were giving a blow-by-blow account live on the radio. Little did I know that the coach and my teammates were listening to the radio and heard the whole thing. Even though Coach would never approve of such behaviour, he was quietly pleased I had come out on top. I managed to escape being fined because I waited until the game was over. Once again, I found a way to play by my own rules.

The 1976 training camp was one of the hardest I ever attended. They had some amazing guys trying out for only a few positions. This was my first year in T.O., and even though this was my fourth year in the league, I had to prove myself all over again.

I almost left the first day I arrived after encountering one of the coaches in the dining room. A guy with weird hair, big arms and twigs for legs walked up to me and with the thickest Southern accent said, "How y'all doing, boy?"

Little did I know that this was my defensive coach, Lamar Leachman, nicknamed Ready Ready. I didn't know how ready he was, but I was sure ready to get out of there.

I also didn't realize at the time that he would be without a doubt one of the greatest coaches and men of integrity I ever met. I was his darling of darlings, as he used to call his defensive line, and all of us felt the same way about him.

I would have an experience in my first year as an Argonaut that would confirm why I felt that way about Coach Leachman. We had to really battle for the few available positions. They had guys like Granville Liggins, who had been a huge All American player at Oklahoma and a perennial CFL all star. Jim Corrigal was there, a Canadian and maybe one of the best native-born players ever. There were only two positions open and a whole lot of guys trying for those two spots. I was up for the task and quickly earned the respect of the coaches and the players. As far as Coach Leachman was concerned, I was the best of that bunch.

After banging heads in camp, Eugene Clark, who was from California and had attended UCLA, and I became best friends. Gene and I were roommates for three years. We were the real odd couple. He was Felix and I was Oscar.

Clark was a great cook and a very talented singer. He actually sang the national anthem several times before the game. He was also very private and was married for almost ten years before I found out. Later he became a successful actor and had roles on both television and the big screen. He was also in the stage production of *Cats* and starred as Mufasa in the theatrical production of *The Lion King*. He encouraged me during my football career, often speaking up on my behalf to the media.

Clark also supported me during my second career in real estate after I retired from football and helped propel me toward my current ministry. He would always tease me by calling me Preacher. We both knew this was my true calling.

In 1976 Lou Ferrigno joined us at training camp. He would become the Incredible Hulk on television. He also won a Mr. Universe title and competed against Arnold Schwarzenegger, but at camp he was the Incredible Sulk. He got us into a barrel full of trouble because he couldn't finish many of the drills. At the time, he was in no condition to play football. Nevertheless, he was strong and would often put on weight demonstrations in the gym after practice.

Lou was nice, even though many of the guys made fun of him because of his hearing disability and speech impediment. I don't believe he had ever played football before. He got the last laugh by going to Hollywood and becoming a huge star.

We roomed next to each other at camp and spent quite a bit of time talking. I remember he had enough and packed it in. He didn't show for a meeting, and we went looking for him. We found him walking down the road with his bag. We convinced him to stick around until the final scrimmage.

The Argonauts stayed true to their reputation of signing big names from the States, and in '76 they signed one of the biggest names in football south of the border, A.D., Anthony Davis, the "Argonaut saviour." He had starred at USC and was one of the top players in the old World Football League. The Argos had signed him to a big contract, given him a huge signing bonus plus a Rolls Royce to add to his other one.

I never figured out why he was a bust in Toronto after having such a brilliant career at USC and in the WFL. It seemed he just never fit in.

For example, after practice most of us would kick back and lie around in shorts and T-shirts, and he would show up wearing an expensive suit. When camp broke, we would find an inexpensive place to live, while he lived in a fancy hotel suite.

We would have the last laugh when he showed up with some model types only to realize they had simply been remodelled and recycled, hoping none of us would blow their cover.

We were roommates when we travelled on the road, and so I became a bit more acquainted with him. I did identify with him to some degree because most of my close friends were not teammates.

I was not into drinking or getting high, so I did my own thing. I got to know a few guys, like Wally Highsmith and Ron Foxx, both Americans. Foxx is now probably better known for dating Shannon Tweed, a Canadian girl who went on to become a Playboy playmate of the year and the wife of Gene Simmons of Kiss fame. More recently the two and their two children have starred in the reality television series *Gene Simmons Family Jewels*.

We would often go out after practice to get something to eat; otherwise I would be with a girlfriend. We all ended up living in a walk-up apartment building not far from the stadium.

The Argonauts were trash talkers
And a real cocky bunch
But as Tiger Cats
We ate them for lunch
They had flash and cash
We had Mosca and the Fly
Before the Grey Cup game
We had passed them by.

NINETEEN

A WALK ON THE DARK SIDE

"The serpent deceived me, and I ate" (Genesis 3:13 NIV).

While I managed to stay away from alcohol, weed, cocaine and other hard drugs, from time to time I would take a benny, which was an upper, to get me primed for a game. Most of the guys who took them would get a prescription from a doctor and pick them up at the local pharmacy.

One afternoon after practice was over, I began to freak out. I never took a benny before practice, only before games, so I thought somehow someone had drugged me. While walking back to my place, I was completely disoriented, although I remember walking up to a high fence. Witnesses said I jumped over the fence, landing flatfooted. The angle and impact of the jump caused me to pull a muscle in my groin.

I had left practice at four that afternoon and walked around for about 24 hours before making my way back to my apartment. I walked for miles with that pulled groin muscle while carrying my playbook under my arm.

I also remember walking on Lakeshore Blvd. east of the Exhibition Stadium, then turning onto Yonge Street past Bloor Street and then onto University Ave. I eventually found my way to Toronto General Hospital. While waiting for someone to help me, I called Mamma, who tried to calm me down, telling me to remain at the hospital.

However, when the doctor got around to looking at me, I was exhibiting a lot of paranoid behaviour. I remember the nurses tried to give me some pills, and I freaked and ran out of the hospital. It was about three in the morning, and I headed towards the bus station on Bay St. I was going to get on the bus but changed my mind and instead kept walking. I remember seeing police, but they didn't stop me.

131

OUR FATHER: THE PRODIGAL SON RETURNS

I finally managed to make my way back to my apartment, in Parkdale. By then, I had missed practice.

I was up for several hours and remember hallucinating while looking out the window. I also remember walking over to the store and buying some water, but I was afraid to drink it.

I hadn't eaten or drank anything for more than 24 hrs.

Finally, I fell asleep, only to be awoken by a loud bang on the door. Someone from the team had come by to check on me. I was a mess.

It didn't take long for the rumours to circulate that I had overdosed on drugs. It even made headlines in the sports section. We had a game in two days, but I couldn't play. I could hardly walk.

I called home, and Mamma and my stepfather hopped on a plane and came to see me. By then I had checked into the Skyline Hotel, owned by Bill Hodgson, the same guy who owned the Argonauts. I had gone for more than 48 hours without eating or drinking a thing. When Mamma and my stepfather arrived, I finally had my first drink and something to eat. I wouldn't touch it, however, until my stepfather tasted it and assured me it was safe.

Next, we had to meet with Dick Shatto, general manager for the Argonauts. J. I. Albrecht, who had brought me in, was there with Russ Jackson, the head coach at the time.

My parents and I assured them I wasn't taking drugs. During the meeting, Lamar showed up. He also told them I wasn't into drugs and that if I said someone drugged me, then that's what happened. He really defended me and made it clear he believed me.

I didn't play in the next game, but I knew I was a valuable member of that team.

Shortly after that affair, I began to attend chapel services before the games but wasn't ready to make a commitment to follow Christ. I was still into a lot of stuff I knew God didn't approve of. There weren't many Christians on the team, and from what I could see only a few of them walked the walk, so I felt fine just going to chapel.

Then I met Mel Stevens, the team chaplain. Mel was a real dude who reminded me of Cool Hand Luke, a character played by Paul Newman in a movie of the same name. Mel was a cowboy, always dressed in a cowboy hat and boots. He made me feel welcome at the chapel services and never pressured me.

After a while, I was calling him Mellow Mel, and he called me Beautiful

Bruce. Mel did something else that would play an important role in my journey back into the light.

He gave all the players on the team a Bible. Mel really understood athletes and knew how vain we were. He gave each of us a Bible with a football helmet, the letter A for Argonaut and our name on it.

I kept that Bible for over 20 years before I opened it. I kept it, not because of what was in it, but because my name was on it. I never took another benny after that incident. I found out I could get that extra adrenaline by having a few cups of coffee.

Taking bennies opened the door
To the evil one
And before I knew it
He had me on the run
I never knew who drugged me
But it wasn't the devil
He had a helper in the locker room
And not from heaven.

TWENTY

LIFE IN THE FAST LANE

Now the men of Sodom were wicked and were sinning greatly against the LORD (Genesis 13:13 NIV).

Coach Lamar asked me to switch from my normal position as defensive tackle to defensive end. I balked at the suggestion but played it, and to my surprise, I discovered it was the position I handled best. I began to appreciate and trust Coach Leachman.

In spite of having one of the top defences in the league, we missed the playoffs. As usual, I headed back to Vancouver, but this time by car via Texas and California.

I always wanted to drive up the coast of California. I decided I would also visit my real father again, plus see my older brother William, who was living in Orange County, south of Los Angeles, not far from Anthony Davis' place.

I spent some time with William and then went to visit AD at his home. While I enjoyed my visit in '76, this time I just felt embarrassed, watching him threaten a guy simply for leaning against his Rolls, which he had parked in front of a club.

The ultimate party animal, he also took me to a club in Westwood where celebrities hung out, including O. J. Simpson, whom I had met in Hawaii along with my childhood idol Jim Brown.

Hanging out with AD was an education. Through him, I learned about the exchange program. They would exchange amongst each other and visiting teams the phone numbers of women who hung out in clubs looking for celebrities.

All of us had the same mindset. Our focus was on pleasing ourselves, and often that meant more pain than pleasure for the women involved. The crazy thing was, many of the girls who came around were no different. Everyone was using everyone, trying to meet needs that none of us could meet. That's what iniquity and unmet needs do: they drive you to self-gratifying actions that often harm you as well as others.

My time in the CFL reminded me a lot of Colorado. There were girls everywhere, and being a football hero, I had many perks. We didn't stand in line at clubs, and whenever we went out, there was always lots of action; we were usually the main attraction. It didn't really matter what team I played for; the off-the-field activities were always the same. Different places, different faces, but the same old script. I think the expression for it is vanity driven by iniquity.

I had the most fun in the CFL during my first year in Hamilton and my third year in Edmonton. Of course, being a starter and an integral part of a winning team is exciting. However, we were like a family, and that's what I enjoyed the most.

George and I were like twins. We would often go out wearing our famous leather suits. I enjoyed spending time with him and his wife, Nancy. They had been high school sweethearts and seemed inseparable. They also had two sons, little George and Jason. Sadly, little George was hit by a car and died. George never really talked about it much, and I often wonder if that's what triggered his drug use. He eventually became a crack addict after finishing his football career.

I always thought George had this drug thing under control, but when crack came on the scene, he really got messed up. I know this is one of the reasons he never made it to the pinnacle in pro wrestling. He had it all, size and ability.

In the mid-eighties, George came to Toronto to wrestle at Maple Leaf Gardens. It was a stacked card, including Andre the Giant, the real Junk Yard Dog and Hulk Hogan. I had the guys over to my house after the match for a party. After several hours, most of them left except George and Junk Yard Dog. They were there with my girlfriend and me. We were all in the master bedroom. That was the first time I saw George do crack. He and the Dog were taking turns doing hits from this glass pipe. Neither my girlfriend nor I did drugs, so we were clueless and didn't think much of it.

Little did I know that this would be the beginning of the end of George's career in wrestling and the end of his marriage to Nancy and, worse yet, soon after the end of Junk Yard Dog's life in a car accident. George eventually lost his family and almost his life while spending years on the streets of Oakland as a crack addict. Thank God, he apparently managed to turn things around and start a new life clean.

LIFE IN THE FAST LANE

In two of my years playing for the Argonauts, I roomed with a guy named Eugene Clark. We lived in the west end and then in a condo called Lambton Square, bordering the Lambton golf course. Until this point, we didn't know downtown Toronto very well. We were both involved in relationships and had somewhat left the club scene. I wasn't out every night anymore. However, I still found time to entertain friends. The truth is, my behaviour hadn't really changed much. By this time, I had a girlfriend in practically every city we played.

In 1977 I came to Toronto early to play in the CFL all-star game representing the Eastern All Stars. It was supposed to be my year. George had also made the team, representing the Western All Stars. I was in peak condition and was ready to claim the title as top defensive lineman in the league.

I had a monster game, which included a couple of sacks, plus I forced a key fumble that would lead to a victory for us. I was the cinch to win the MVP award alone with a beautiful trophy and prize, but to everyone's shock, I was overlooked again. Although I was disappointed, I had gotten used to this kind of thing.

In training camp, I quickly established myself as the top defensive lineman, which Coach Leachman confirmed in an article in the *Toronto Star*. It became more apparent after the annual blue and white scrimmage.

Toronto had signed Nick Bastaja, who had been an all-star offensive tackle for Hamilton. I put a beating on him so bad he wanted to quit. I went over at lunch to encourage him by saying he just had an off day. We became best friends after that.

I really had it all going for me, and it appeared I was finally going to get the recognition I deserved for being one of the best, if not the best, at that time. However, as fate would have it, I was injured in a fluke accident when my teammate got hit in a game and fell backward on my knee.

After only a couple of games I would end up missing the rest of the season, having surgery on both knees and spending 28 weeks on crutches, including part of the off-season in Vancouver.

We travelled to Vancouver that year to play against the BC Lions, and the team let me travel with them to Vancouver. My friend who owned the club where I worked and hung out came to pick me up at the airport in his vintage white Bentley.

Back in Vancouver in the off-season, I worked in a club called Misty's while I prepared for another season in Toronto. There was no shortage of entertainment as Misty's was across the street from the famous nightclub The Cave, a real den of iniquity.

The year 1978 would be a difficult one for the Argonauts and more difficult for me, because Coach Lamar had moved to Montreal. Replacing him would be another "good ol' boy," named Dell White. They also brought in Bud Riley, an Alabama guy who could have been his twin. They definitely wore the same uniform. I felt like I was back in Texas. I never had a good feeling about them, and I know they felt the same about me.

Management brought back Leo Cahill, a very colourful coach who had been the last to take the team to the Grey Cup championship, in 1971. I liked Leo and was one of his favourites, but I didn't want to have anything to do with the Bud and Dell show.

Even though I was having a good year, we were losing again. The place was like Grand Central Station with them trying to find the right combination of American and Canadian players.

We had been so hopeful things would be different that year. That was the year after Toronto signed the "Georgia connection," Mike Wilson and Joel Parrish, two all Americans from the Georgia Bull Dogs, and outstanding cornerback Eric Harris. They also signed one of the top running backs in the NFL, Terry Metcalf of the St. Louis Cardinals.

With all that talent, we still lost. To make matters worse, now I didn't like the coach, and he didn't like me. It wasn't long before we began to sing a song the coach had heard before, "Goodbye, Leo" and before you knew it, he was fired again. Then the thing I dreaded most happened; they replaced Leo with Bud, and of course, old Dell was in his glory. I know if it was up to him, I would have been on my way out with Leo. However, that didn't happen.

Things got a bit nasty when they announced the nominees for the team's outstanding player award and, in spite of having a better season than any other defensive lineman, I was not put forward by him. I went ballistic and spoke about racism in a *Toronto Star* interview. I figured after that I was a goner, that there was no way I would be back in '79. Well they did make a change, but it wasn't me. They fired the coach, and the Bud and Dell team was history. I remember thinking there must really be a God up there in heaven.

Very early in the off-season, they announced they had signed NFL legend Forrest Gregg, a former player for arguably the best coach in the history of football, Vince Lombardi. I had mixed emotions; on the one hand, I was excited to play for someone with his pedigree, but on the other, it meant starting over at first base to prove myself again. I had a chance to meet Coach Gregg, and he assured me that he had plans for me for the upcoming season and that I would be given every chance to compete for my job.

This would also be my last off-season in Vancouver. You might say I burned a few bridges before I left.

It was like back in The Alley with Bud and Dell
And I didn't want to spend another season in hell.

TWENTY-ONE

THE BEST FOR LAST

You may be the heavyweight champion of the world.
You may be a socialite with a long string of pearls.
But you're gonna have to serve somebody, yes indeed
Well, it may be the devil or it may be the Lord
But you're gonna have to serve somebody.
"Gotta Serve Somebody," by Bob Dylan
Copyright © 1979 by Special Rider Music

I would spend the next off-season in Toronto preparing for the 1979 season as an Argonaut.

That off-season my friend Eugene convinced me to lift weights and really go all out preparing. We joined a local gym with several of our teammates, including Larry Bray, Gord Knowlton and Rick Sowvietta.

We worked hard lifting and running, and by the time training rolled around I had gained about 10 pounds of muscle and increased my endurance by doing sprints and running three miles three to four times per week. As they say, I was a welcome sight and an unholy terror. This was going to be our year, and we started the season looking like we would be the front-runners for the coveted Holy Grail, the Grey Cup.

Everyone was talking about Toronto, especially the front four, our defensive line. I was singled out as the designated leader, the top dog. It seemed I was finally going to get the respect and recognition that had eluded me. I was named one of the co-captains along with Terry and my new road dog Nick Bastasia, whom we called Disco Nick.

"You shall worship the LORD your God, and Him only you shall serve"

OUR FATHER: THE PRODIGAL SON RETURNS

(Matthew 4:10 NKJV). It seemed I had finally gotten it together. I was living larger than life with my off-the-field activities. I had heads turning and tongues wagging and was driving a new Mercedes Benz. All this and I wasn't even taking any of my salary.

But I was surrounded by darkness. I thought I was in control, not realizing whoever controls the flesh controls the rest. I was totally out of control, living only to please myself. I cared about self and no one else. I was serving the god of self-worshipping Satan, not the Lord. I was self-seeking, self-indulgent, sailing down that famous Egyptian river called De Nile. I had no idea we all are serving somebody, and it's either the devil or the Lord. Well, the Lord is the light, and we live in the light by walking in the truth. I was living a lie, so I definitely was not serving the Lord.

I had a Bible and went to chapel before the games, but in reality I was a card-carrying Satan worshiper, one of the devil's poster boys. Even though I still believed in the Lord, I wasn't ready to trust Him.

I had gotten into the club scene in uptown Toronto and was a regular at a bar called Rooneys, among others. As usual, there were long lines, but we walked in like we owned the place.

While the '79 season ended with us missing the playoffs and me missing the last game because of a knee injury, it was a good year for me. I made the coaches all star at defensive end instead of defensive tackle, as I had the year before. I was also nominated as the Argonauts' defensive player of the year.

I literally crawled off the field after the last play in a game against the Tiger Cats. I went directly to the hospital after the game and was scheduled for surgery the next morning. I ended up back in Vancouver for a few weeks before training camp to visit a physiotherapist named Alex, who worked wonders getting my leg strong enough to play for a few more seasons.

The off-season would bring another surprise. After signing a contract to stay in Toronto, Coach Gregg opted out to take the head-coaching job at the Cincinnati Bengals. I was surprised and disappointed like a lot of people, because he had pledged his allegiance to the Argonauts.

When they announced his replacement, many people were surprised. It was Willie Woods, who had come to Toronto with him. Like a lot of people I was happy, because Willie would become the first black coach of a professional football team.

After meeting with him in the off-season we had a difference of opinion about what position I would play, so I refused to report to training camp. After giving it some thought I decided it was time to retire. They released me in the end, but that was academic, because I had already decided to pack it in. It was a decision I never regretted and still don't today.

The season started on a high
But ended with a low blow
I would never don the double blue anymore
Another chapter was over, I turned the page
It was time to move on because of age.

TWENTY-TWO

TURNING THE PAGE

Listen, my son, to your father's instruction and do not forsake your mother's teaching. They will be a garland to grace your head and a chain to adorn your neck (Proverbs 1:8–9 NIV).

Although I was happy with my decision to retire from football, I also realized I could have accomplished much more had I not been a lost soul. As a college and professional player I had been defined as talented, but unfortunately also a troublemaker, a "rebel" who was disruptive to team chemistry and continuity.

I now realize that part of my rebellion had its roots in my not having a father in my life. It was great to have "father figures" like my high school coach, Mr. McGee, and Jerry Williams, my coach in Hamilton, but neither of them was my father, and there were many things I couldn't share with them.

Furthermore, while I honoured and respected them for reaching out and helping me, it was impossible for them as white authority figures to comprehend and deal with the issues I faced as a young black male in a white-dominated world. How could they really understand how I felt, not having faced or lived under the oppression of Jim Crow and death row? Being told almost daily that you can't sit here, eat here, walk here or live here. I needed a strong black father who could dispense wisdom and knowledge to me in the same way King David did for Solomon, imparting those proverbs as well as life lessons, which made him "the wisest man in the world." Where was my King David, the overriding tower of strength who would encourage, correct and support me in my journey to manhood?

There was never the right man to mentor me in my formative years, to provide the right modelling, so I became my own mentor. I became the person others followed. Madness when you think about it, because what this represented was the blind leading the blind.

This was not only my reality; it was the case for my other black teammates and friends. As a result, we relied on our knowledge and wisdom, which was close to zero. It's difficult to make wise decisions as a man when you have not been mentored and taught as a son.

This accounts for a lot of the foolish and reckless decisions we made. We didn't know better.

Let's face it, who could I talk to about what to do and what to avoid? Mothers, particularly black mothers, are amazing, but my mother and many mothers are not equipped to deal with head coaches and pro football general managers. As stated earlier, I had seen my stepfather totally humiliated by his white boss, and so no one in my world back in The Alley could help me deal with what I was facing.

I see a father as a leader, an authority figure doling out love, affection and discipline in appropriate measures. He is the one to turn to in times of trial and the one you long to please. This is critical for young people, regardless of their race or gender. They need men who are real fathers. The chances of males growing up to be nurturing fathers increase significantly when they have a good role model for a father.

At this point in my life, thirty-one years old and finished playing football, I turned my attention to self-reliance. To the outside world, I was a success, a former All-Pro and team captain on the verge of starting a successful business, but internally I was still missing the fundamentals, "the proverbs" handed down from a father to a son.

> *King Solomon was taught by his father*
> *King David*
> *But all I learned from my fathers*
> *Was rejection and failure*
> *Soon I would have a wise Father too*
> *Who would love me unconditionally and teach me what to do*
> *Without a real father, I didn't understand*
> *You need a good role model to be a good man.*

TWENTY-THREE

EXPANDING MY LAND

"Oh, that you would bless me and enlarge my territory!"
(1 Chronicles 4:10 NIV).

Having played football from age six to thirty-two, it was time for a new career. I had two ideas, to become a stockbroker or a real estate agent.

I had recently invested a nice chunk of money in the stock market through a friend in Vancouver, but the combination of his inexperience and my greed ended in disaster. I lost everything. The stock market was strong in 1980 and had continued to go up the first few months of 1981. The same thing was happening in the real estate market, so I decided to buy my first home in Toronto. I bought a two-year-old townhouse in a place called Cabbagetown.

This was the beginning of a love affair with buying and selling real estate. The couple who had the listing on the place was old and apparently successful. I used a retired teammate who had moved into real estate part-time to handle the deal.

After figuring out how much commission my teammate had made, I was convinced that this was the career for me. I sold the house after being there for just over a year and made a little profit. I used an agent, and she encouraged me to try a career in real estate.

From time to time I had considered real estate as a career, because Mamma had worked for a family whose son went into real estate and did well. She often encouraged me by telling me about the nice clothes and beautiful cars he always drove. I was still in high school at the time, but she was convinced I had what it took to succeed. She would say, "Bruce, you are every bit as smart as Bill Terrell, and I believe you would do real good in real estate." I don't know how she knew, but she was right.

OUR FATHER: THE PRODIGAL SON RETURNS

In the fall of 1980, I signed up for the real estate course, a five-week eight-hour-a-day course. It was a lot of work, but this was what I wanted. I was willing to put in the time to study and go to class. I ended up passing all the way through the first time with no rewrites. By the time I took all the courses and wrote the exams, it was spring 1981.

FROM THE ALLEY TO FOREST HILL

Shortly after completing my course in real estate, I decided to visit different offices to see where I might fit in. I wasn't familiar with Toronto and had never heard of Forest Hill. I still don't know how I ended up there.

There were a number of real estate offices on one of the main streets, Eglinton Ave. I went into all of them; however, the one person who made time for me was Paul Slavens, one of the top brokers in the area. Slavens is Jewish, and I think all of his agents at the time were Jewish. He gave me a lot of good advice, including suggesting that I go to a major firm, take career development classes and learn as much as I could before deciding on an office. I took his advice, joined a major national firm and entered their career development program.

After meeting their criteria of making a sale and getting a couple of listings, I was ready to find a permanent place to work. I decided to stay with the company, given that they had invested time and money in training me. The firm had two outstanding offices within a few miles of each other. Wouldn't you know it, they sent me to the one on Eglinton Ave, only four blocks from Paul Slavens Real Estate.

I am sure with hindsight he wouldn't have helped me if he realized that within a few years of our first meeting I would be one of the top agents and brokers in the area. My presence in the neighbourhood cost him thousands and thousands in commissions, as well as headaches for him and many of his agents.

Not long after I arrived at my new office, the manager asked where I'd like to focus my sales efforts. "What's the name of the area around the office?" I asked.

"Forest Hill," he said.

"Well, according to my instruction manual I should specialize in an area close to my office." I decided I would work in Cedarvale, which is next door to Forest Hill, one of the wealthiest neighbourhoods in Toronto.

The manager was surprised at my response and commented that the area was Jewish and in so many words suggested this was probably not a good career decision.

EXPANDING MY LAND

It was April 1981, and the real estate market and stock market were taking a nosedive. Interest rates shot up to 22 percent, and the market was flooded with houses. Very little was selling.

I went through the motions that year. Then in 1982 I had a wake-up call. I woke up at 5 a.m. and decided that I would be the number one agent in my office. At the time, I wasn't even on the industry radar screen.

I got up, went to the office and wrote on the sales board "Bruce Smith #1." The market was still in a downward spiral, but I was determined to follow through. I didn't end up number one that year, but I sold enough to earn an award trip to Martinique.

By 1983 I was the top agent in that office of forty-five agents, mostly Jewish. Four of them were some of the national company's most successful agents. Shortly after I became the number one producer, and they all left for other offices.

My production would almost double every year until 1987, when I became the company's top producer and among the top three or four agents for the company in all of Canada.

Now I was more like the prodigal son when he left home. I had fame and success way beyond anyone's expectations, including my own. I could go where I wanted, do what I wanted, and all I wanted increasingly was pleasure. The more I earned, the more I could indulge myself. Like with any addiction, the more you have, the more you try to meet those unmet needs.

I was the most recognized realtor in the area, which wasn't very hard, because there were no other 6'2" 275 pound real estate agents who were black, driving a Mercedes with a "Bear 61" (my football number) vanity plate, wearing a full length otter coat, and selling homes to mostly Jewish people. I was also involved in some seriously wild living. It would be years before I came to my senses.

In the fall of 1986, I decided to get my broker's licence. It was obvious to everyone that my success had very little to do with the company. In fact, they had not really given me much help. I began to resent being there, and I didn't have very much respect for the manager either. When any of the other agents needed help with listings or deals, they would often come to me for advice. However, in hindsight I realize the problem wasn't him but me.

I was doing my own thing, playing by my own rules, with no regard for authority. I wanted to leave, and yet I was afraid to leave my comfort zone. I became angry and more resentful and showed no regard for the other agents and no respect for the manager.

OUR FATHER: THE PRODIGAL SON RETURNS

In the fall of 1987, about two months after being honoured as the top agent in Toronto for the company, I was fired. Naturally, I was extremely angry and wanted to sue for wrongful dismissal, but in reality, it was the best thing that could have happened to me.

I went on a tear for about three weeks, and when it was over, I had gotten my broker's licence, started my own company right across the street from my former office and gotten engaged. I also went out and bought a Rolls Royce, but the dealer reneged on the deal, so I settled for a new Mercedes.

I bought a different house and had it renovated, designed a new image and logo for my company and had my new office refurbished. I got fired at the right time because the market was about to go up about 40 percent, and I had lots of listings and lots of clients. I decided to have a grand opening with catered food and music, and to top it off I had most of the guests picked up by limo. It was the talk of the street. We also had bear wear, which included hats, T-shirts and sweatshirts with our Panda logo. We gave stuffed pandas to our clients' children. We spared no expense. The sales were rolling in, and I didn't have to split with anyone.

My life at this time reminds me of what I heard about the lives of rock stars. My success in sales had catapulted me to the top in real estate. My personal life however was completely out of control. Imagine trying to manage people when I couldn't even manage my own life.

My success in real estate thrilled me because it was totally unexpected and in a completely different field. There was no previous indication that inside me was a natural born salesman. Selling real estate would bring out the hidden side of me, the ability to persuade people and to promote myself.

During most of my years in football, I was labeled a troublemaker, and I had a reputation for being unpredictable, withdrawn and introverted. Imagine the shock when the reports began to surface concerning my success and great reputation in the real estate business. There is no such thing as an introverted successful real estate agent. No. Selling is persuading and promoting yourself as well as the properties you are trying to buy or sell to people. I earned a reputation as one of the best.

No one could have predicted how successful I would become. I earned enough plaques and awards to fill a whole room. If there was an all-star real estate team, I was the most valuable player.

After I became a broker and had my own company, I actually paid more in income taxes than I earned as a professional in the Canadian Football League.

EXPANDING MY LAND

I had my own team. I was the owner, the coach and the most valuable player, and everyone had to play by my rules.

I was also my own referee. All of us have a built-in referee called our conscience. God gave all of us one to know right from wrong. However, many people like me ignore the warnings until they can no longer hear them.

I had learned to ignore
The voice inside me
Not realizing
It was the voice
Of my own spirit
Warning me.
Even when it got louder
I still ignored
And was about to experience
The judgment sword.

TWENTY-FOUR

THE TEXAS TORNADO TOUCHES DOWN IN TORONTO

"I will mock when calamity overtakes you—
when calamity overtakes you like a storm, when disaster sweeps
over you like a whirlwind" (Proverbs 1:26–27 NIV).

I was finally on my own, with no one to answer to except myself. I could come and go as I pleased. However, in reality not much had changed. I was still full of pride and anger, and it didn't take much to set me off.

I was back in business with a vengeance, and if anyone crossed me, vengeance was mine.

When I look back, I can only say, "What was I thinking? I must have been out of my mind!"

In a sense I was, because many of my decisions were influenced by unmet needs and unseen iniquity. Rather than being led by a sound mind, I was often led by unstable emotions. Anger influenced many of my decisions, and I often controlled and intimidated people with anger. Other times I would lose control, verbally and emotionally abusing others. When I got started there was no stopping me until I had the object of my wrath in tears.

Way before the term *road rage* was first used, I was involved in a number of incidents. On a number of occasions I chased people who cut me off, cornering them and giving them a piece of my mind. I even took road rage to a whole new level, chasing people at high speeds until I caught them, ripping off their windshield wipers and kicking in their windows. Now that I can reflect, I see unresolved issues brought on by my anger, many of which can be traced to the pain and disappointment I felt as a child, teenager and young adult because of being rejected by my father.

While I acted out with violence and promiscuity, many people try to cover up feelings of rejection and disappointment and end up with cancer or ulcers. We either express it or depress it. One way leads to destroying yourself; the other leads to destroying yourself and others, which is very selfish.

The Texas tornado that chased me west to Colorado had made a sharp northeasterly turn to Toronto. I had escaped the restrictive environment of The Alley years earlier, but the seeds from fatherlessness planted in my youth had produced ugly fruits of anger, hostility, cruelty, greed and unforgiveness. It might have been calm and cool outside in the Great White North, but inside me, a hot southern twister was building.

My erratic behaviour on the roads eventually led to my being charged with assault with the use of a car. My friend George Wells and I were headed uptown to our favourite club, Rooneys, when a white guy cut me off and flipped us the old birdie. He made the mistake of saying what we thought were racist comments.

My mind flashed back to that day when I saw my stepfather, Ernest, humiliated by his boss, Ol' Man Reiner, the day he bragged to his friends "That's my nigger!" pointing to my stepfather. I felt I was now in a position to right an old wrong.

I couldn't have done anything about it in Huntsville, Texas, in the early sixties as a boy in a man's world. Now, as a grown ex All-Pro ball player and a young real estate mogul, living in Toronto, in my mind, the tables had turned. Now I could do something about it, and throwing discretion and caution to the wind, I determined that I would.

We chased him all the way up Yonge Street at ridiculously high speeds, at times tailgating him so close that I eventually rear-ended him. In an effort to escape us, he pulled over by a club and jumped out of his car, fleeing through the door. I wasn't going to let him get away, so I parked outside to wait for him.

As we sat there, a cop car pulled up. Someone had called the police, maybe from the manager's office where we later found out he was hiding. Not only was I charged for the accident, I was charged with assault and had to pay a lawyer to defend me. The bill always comes in for wrong behaviour, and sometimes the price is jail, loss of loved ones and sometimes even loss of life.

The year 1988 was big in many ways. First, it was the biggest in sales and commissions, and second, it was a year of unprecedented spending. I was definitely having a love affair with the world and things of the world. There were $20,000 shopping sprees. It was not uncommon for me to spend thousands of dollars on expensive diamonds and gold watches. At one point, I had a different watch for every day of the week.

THE TEXAS TORNADO TOUCHES DOWN IN TORONTO

This would be the year when the agent who started with me just one year earlier would purchase a $10,000 Rolex and trade up to a Mercedes Benz.

Our first child was born that year, and naturally, she had to have the best of everything. Her birth showed me that God has a sense of humour. Our first child was a girl and looked just like me.

Even some of my clients suggested her name should have been Brucia. We decided on Courtne instead. I was totally unprepared for this, and while I provided everything she needed financially, I was often absent physically and emotionally.

Here I was with a beautiful wife, Shirley, and daughter, home, successful business, all the trappings of success and still unfulfilled. I figured as long as I provided materially for them I was fulfilling my duty as a husband and a father. I was providing more than my father had provided me. At least I was there.

This is exactly the kind of thinking I now hope to change. It takes a lot more than living under the same roof and paying the bills to be a father. A healthy father is one who is there emotionally, spiritually and physically. He is there to provide and protect; he is there to care and share.

During this volatile spell, there were some good times. We shared a lot of great moments with close friends and with the children. We visited our friends in their homes, and they visited us. We also went on several trips every year and always took Courtne. But what should have been the best time of my life was marred by anger and strife and self-centredness.

I started buying investment properties to flip them for a quick profit. It was business as usual at the office. We managed to keep turning a profit, even though I was using a line of credit to service a lot of the mortgage debt from the investment properties.

To top it off, the decisions to invest were made solely by me, so my wife had no clue how much debt I was accumulating. After all, I was the sole provider, so the provisions were mine to do with as I pleased, in my opinion.

The year 1992 would be our best. By now we had our second child, Coby, a son, which in a way I hoped would be the beginning of a turning point.

It was a turning point all right, but in the wrong direction. I still lived in darkness. The warning bells began to ring a little louder and with more frequency, but I wasn't ready to stop and listen.

The first one came in what I thought was a heart attack. I quietly checked myself into the hospital and stayed overnight for tests, only to be told I was suffering from anxiety. I knew it was more than anxiety, but doctors cannot detect all things.

OUR FATHER: THE PRODIGAL SON RETURNS

Being a good father
Takes more than bringing home provisions
It takes loving your family
And making wise decisions
It takes humility to admit
When you're wrong
It means taking care of business
At work and at home.

TWENTY-FIVE

TURNING POINT

*Let no one be found among you who sacrifices his son or daughter
in the fire, who practices divination or sorcery, interprets omens,
engages in witchcraft, or casts spells, or who is a medium or spiritist
or who consults the dead. Anyone who does these things is detestable
to the LORD* (Deuteronomy 18:10–12 NIV).

Up to this point, I found some satisfaction in what I had accomplished. I had escaped The Alley, Jim Crow and death row. I had overcome adversity and racism in university and had seen my dream of playing professional football materialize by coming to Canada. I had become a superstar in the real estate business and found fame and fortune in 12 years. I had amazed many people, including myself, with my accomplishments as a top salesman and broker.

My life then reminds me of the story of the woman who drank water from a famous well but was always thirsty. She tried religion and spirituality, even going to worship in the mountains where her ancestors went, and yet she was still seeking. She married five times and was now living with another man but remained unfulfilled.

I had taken self-indulgence to new heights, except I didn't get any taller, only a whole lot wider. My weight ballooned up to about three hundred and twenty pounds. I was eating plenty but I was never full. I had spent over twenty-five years feeling sorry for myself, defending myself, indulging myself, promoting myself and being full of myself, and yet something was still missing.

Today I know my behaviour was rooted in my insecurity over growing up black, poor and fatherless in Texas. I was trying to build protective walls to insulate myself from it; becoming a pro athlete and a real estate entrepreneur and accumulating material wealth were all "worldly achievements," and the accolades, I believed, would fill that void. Obviously, they did not.

In 1993, I started getting interested in spiritual things. It is said that what is most important for men before they turn forty is achieving success, but after forty it's all about being significant. That year I knew I wanted something I didn't have, and I knew it wasn't more success or more stuff. I wanted to give something back to society.

I decided one way would be to go to schools and share my success story with young people. An old friend from the eighties helped me get into the schools. I spoke to several hundred thousand students over a rewarding three-year period.

In 1993, my friend Patrick Ryan came to work for my company. He had a friend in Calgary named Les Hewitt who was booking speakers for seminars in his province.

He dared me to go there to speak on the same program with well-known author and public speaker W. Mitchell, a man who escaped death in a fiery plane crash that left him severely deformed. I took the challenge, and we flew to Calgary, where I had my first taste of public speaking. It went fairly well, and Les, Mitchell and Patrick encouraged me to continue speaking.

I began to read a lot of books and listen to tapes of people like Mark Victor Hansen, whom I met in Toronto, and Deepak Chopra, whom I heard speak at a conference I attended with friends and former real estate clients Cheryl Stott and Alex and Dory Korn.

I became a voracious reader of books by Mary Ann Williamson and others on Eastern religion, meditation and New Age spirituality. The funny thing about New Age is that it isn't new. People's quest to be like God or find self-defined routes to heaven, like those who built the Tower of Babel, have been with us since creation.

As I explored the New Age movement and attended the Silva Mind and other conferences, I began to experiment with meditation and eventually trained myself to sit for hours just being quiet and still. Although I felt a sense of calmness, at times I knew I hadn't found what I was looking for.

"My people are destroyed for lack of knowledge" (Hosea 4:6 KJV).

TURNING POINT

INVISIBLE COUNSELLORS

No one likes to admit they're ignorant, but I had no clue about spirituality. Being spiritual to me meant doing good things for others. I admit that doing something good for someone else made me feel great. In all of us, there is the desire to do good. Even hardened criminals do good for others at times.

I discovered through my readings that some spiritualists teach that you don't have to go to church or even read or believe the Bible to be spiritual. In fact, the type of spirituality I was involved in said you could create your own truth as long as it felt good. They called it creating your own reality.

I began to read more and more books on Eastern religion and became a fan of a yogi named Yogananda. The Silva Mind course had taught me to empty my mind, but I would soon learn that I was opening my mind not only to the truth but to much danger and deception. The idea was to open your mind to receive from spiritual guidance the universe, which, I might add, could be demons and wicked spirits disguised as messengers of light. No wonder even Satan himself transforms himself into an *"angel of light"* (2 Corinthians 11:14 NKJV).

I also read the very popular book *Think and Grow Rich*, even though at the time I wasn't after money or riches. My journey through books on spirituality and empowerment gave me many insights, but I had a hard time connecting any human being to unlimited power. Even though I wasn't a Christian or even religious, I knew unlimited power could only belong to God and not man.

This was also when the black version of *Think and Grow Rich* by Dennis Kimbro came on the market. I attended a workshop with him. He was very impressive.

In his book, I read of a man named Alonzo Herndon, a very successful black man who was the founder of Atlanta Life Insurance in Atlanta, Georgia, in the late 1800s. Several things intrigued me about this man. He was black and successful. He apparently used his influence and wealth to help people, especially black people. My Uncle Beji, whose real name was Alonzo, also worked for the Atlanta Life Insurance Company.

The book spoke about "invisible counsellors," which are supposed to represent guidance from the spirits of people who have passed on. I felt that Herndon was supposed to be my invisible counsellor. Therefore I followed the suggestion in the book and set out an empty chair and invited the spirit of this dead man to counsel me. Well, something came in response to my invitation, and I know it wasn't who or what I was expecting.

I would spend hours in the basement meditating and reading. I wasn't the only one sensing something strange in our basement. After that encounter, neither my wife nor my daughter was comfortable being in the basement.

Even though I had no knowledge of spiritual things, I knew instantly that this was something evil. This was the beginning of three weeks of insanity. I went three weeks sleeping most nights only one or two hours, and sometimes I would be up for twenty-four hrs.

At times I felt calm, and at other times there was a surge of power. It was as if I could read someone's mind and was being led to places to help others.

A friend in real estate had lost her daughter, and for no reason I called her office to speak to her and found out she was not there. I immediately had a sense something was wrong and showed up at her doorstep. Not long after I sat on her couch, her cat came over and sat on my lap.

She told me this was where her daughter used to sit when she came downstairs and that the cat was hers. Apparently, the cat would only sit in that particular place when her daughter sat there and had been upstairs since her daughter passed away.

Another night I was driving a friend of my wife's home after she visited. As I came to a stoplight about two blocks from my office, I heard a voice say, "Move to this vacant space."

Within several days, I announced we were moving to a larger space.

There were more signs. Tony Robbins was in town for a seminar. I had this immense desire to see him, and I didn't know why. I went to his conference, arriving a little after it started, so I sat at the back. This was his heyday, and the people were pumped. I sat quietly listening and watching. Toward the end of the conference he began to talk about all the good work he did helping the poor. I thought to myself, *This sounds good.*

I decided to leave early to avoid the crowd, but while I was getting my coat, I heard a voice say, "This is not why you are here, Bruce." So I went back inside and waited to speak to Robbins.

Naturally, when the conference was over, several hundred people lined up to get his autograph. I positioned myself near the stage, not knowing which way he would leave or how long I would have to wait. While I was standing there, a woman walked up and whispered in Tony's ear. She then announced that Mr. Robbins had to leave to catch his flight.

He walked off the stage within feet of me, so I stopped him. Staring him in the eye I asked, "Tony, where does unlimited power come from?" I obviously caught him off guard.

I asked him again. He said, "What do you mean?"

Then the look on his face said, "I got it." He nodded and looked upward as if to acknowledge, yes, "unlimited power" comes from a higher power, not man, which was the answer I hoped for.

I was satisfied.

Three weeks later, I hit a wall, realizing I needed help. That night I tried to sleep, but I kept hearing voices outside my bedroom window. As the voices grew louder, I freaked out and ran and grabbed my wife and little Courtne, bringing them by force into the bedroom and onto the bed.

I put my arm over them so they couldn't move. Then I jumped up and ran over to my desk and got that Bible I had carried for over twenty years, putting it under my pillow. Naturally, my wife was freaking out. I remember eventually managing to fall asleep, but only for an hour.

The next day my wife was in the kitchen with a friend, and to their surprise I said, "I think I need some help."

I decided to see a psychiatrist who was a client and had an office at one of the hospitals. I remember walking up to his receptionist and asking for him. She said Dr. Freedman didn't work on Tuesdays, but when we turned to leave, there he was walking into his office. Naturally he was surprised to see me, and I was relieved to see him.

He took us into his office, and I shared some of the experiences I had. I could tell he was concerned. The truth is, I only told him part of what was happening, because I figured he would think I had really lost my mind.

He said, "First of all, you are suffering from sleep deprivation, which can contribute to the behaviour you are experiencing." He gave me two prescriptions, one for sleeping pills and the other for a drug called lithium. We stopped at the pharmacy on the way out and picked up the pills.

When I arrived home, I was not comfortable taking the others, but I took some of the sleeping pills. Finally I fell asleep.

I received a call from Dr. Freedman sometime between 6:30 and 7 a.m., asking how I was doing. I told him I had gotten some sleep, and he asked if I had taken any of the other pills. I hadn't. His said he didn't think I needed them, so I threw them away.

I had no knowledge of spiritual things; however, I surmised that, like with gravity, if we break the laws concerning them we aren't exempt because of our ignorance. God's commands concerning the spirit realm are clearly spelled out in Scripture. Whether we believe them or not or choose to ignore them does not exempt us from being influenced or affected by them. I had unknowingly opened the door to the dark side by doing the very things God had expressly forbidden in Scripture.

Do you ever wonder why God expressly forbade the children of Israel from dabbling in the occult? It's because He knows that there are other spiritual beings besides Him and that we can connect with them through any one of the mediums of the occult, a practice He forbids in Deuteronomy.

Even though God and other spirit beings are invisible, they are not impersonal. God, angels and demons have personalities like human beings have; however, they are just a whole lot smarter and more powerful, with God being the wisest and most powerful being in the universe. Only God is all powerful, all wise, all knowing, and all present.

I have learned from this spiritual quest that there is good and evil. God is good, and Satan is evil, and one or the other influences our choices. Supernatural power is not necessarily from God. Much of what we think is supernatural power is actually demonic power, and behind demonic power is the devil.

Satan has powers we mortals don't have, and we can tap into these to accomplish worldly goals, like acquiring great wealth, success, celebrity and even healing. However, never forget that the ultimate purpose of Satan is to keep you away from the truth, which is found in Christ. Satan hates God and all human beings whom God loves. Satan knows he can't get to God, so he goes after what God loves and wants most, and that is to have an intimate relationship with you and spend eternity with you. Satan has one goal, and that is to keep you away from knowing God. Satan wants nothing more than for you to spend eternity away from God with him and his demons, and he will offer you anything to accomplish his goal.

The devil is a liar and a thief and will offer you counterfeit power. He comes only *"to steal, and to kill, and to destroy"* (John 10:10 NKJV), and he will use our desires and unmet needs to keep us from the one thing we need the most, a personal and intimate relationship with God.

All human beings are subject to higher powers. Either we choose God, the Father of truth, or the devil, the father of liars.

TURNING POINT

I don't believe
All paths lead to heaven
Any more than 666 equals 7
The devil will try
And counterfeit everything God does
Because he is no longer
The top angel he once was
He is a cheap imitation
A lousy fake
That's why he's called
Lord of flies
And a slimy snake.

TWENTY-SIX

REPENTANCE, MAKING A U-TURN

"I will arise and go to my father, and will say to him, 'Father, I have sinned against heaven and before you'" (Luke 15:18 NKJV).

"Repent, for the kingdom of heaven is near" (Matthew 4:17 NIV).

In the fall of 1993, I was managing an open house in upper Forest Hill and for some reason took my Argonaut Bible with me. It wasn't very busy, so I decided to read it.

I flipped it open to the book of Luke, to the story of John the Baptist. I remember thinking that this dude sounded a little like me, except he had both a mother and a father. At the time, I was still wearing my full-length otter coat. Interestingly, the Bible described John the Baptist as eccentric and dressed in a camel's hair coat.

The Scripture also said he didn't drink, and neither did I. Reading this piqued my curiosity. Then I read that he would *"turn many of the children of Israel to the Lord their God"* (Luke 1:16 NKJV). I immediately thought of my friends Alex, Dory and Cheryl, who were Jewish but, like most of the Jews I knew, were secular and like me knew something about religion but really nothing about God.

The Scripture also said that he would *"turn the hearts of the fathers to the children"* (Luke 1:17 NKJV), and immediately I thought about my own children.

The only difference between me, a secular Gentile, and the secular Jews I knew was that they went to the synagogue on high holidays and would usually have a bar mitzvah for their sons, and we limited our church experiences to Christmas, Easter and having our children christened.

After reading the Bible, I reasoned if I were truly a seeker I should at least attend church. So to my wife's surprise I said, "Let's go to church." She has a friend named Nellie who attended a little Anglican church called St Chad's, so we decided to go there.

I decided I would go once a month. Frankly, I decided to go there because the services were no more than an hour, and not a lot of people went.

Soon we were going twice a month, and then every week. After about six months, something happened that I wouldn't fully understand until several years later. I began to feel deep sorrow for my negative attitudes and behaviour. That's the power of God's Word.

The little church I attended was quiet, with the expected WASPy reserve you would expect at The Church of England, and the sermons and preaching were not very moving. But the Holy Spirit was moving, because the liturgies were God's Word and the sacraments honoured the atoning and redeeming work of Christ.

The more I went to the church, the more I began to feel remorseful about all the people I had hurt, especially my wife. I began to change the company I kept and the places I went. I also began to talk about God a lot in my office. People started to feel uncomfortable, and some left.

It was now 1994, and three of my closest friends had become committed Christians. My secretary, Beverly, was a committed Christian, and so was Eugene Clark, who began giving me Christian books and tapes.

The other two who helped me find Christ were Margaret Parker and Chris Hinn. According to Marg, my first comment when I heard that she had accepted Christ was "He got you too!" Apparently, they spent a great deal of time praying for me.

I was still confused in my personal life and really thought a change would be better for everyone. Change came, but not in the way I had in mind. I had come close to changing partners, but I decided to pray about it.

God began to remove temptation out of the way. I knew it was God because I had prayed earnestly. This time I was ready. I had experienced first-hand the mercy, grace and power of God.

I knew I needed to respond to God's outstretched hand, and the response was to repent, to make a U-turn, which meant a change of mind and attitude toward sin and God but most of all a change of heart, which only God can inspire.

I followed the example of the prodigal son and confessed my sins against God and against the people I hurt and invited Christ into my heart.

It was like someone had taken this big weight off my shoulders. I had finally discovered what I had really longed for, and that was peace, a sense of purpose and joy.

God put me on the right path to peace and purpose, and there were no more detours.

I read a psalm written by King David after he had confessed and repented of his sins that really expressed how I felt after confessing my sins to God and repenting. *"What joy for those whose disobedience is forgiven, whose sin is put out of sight! Yes, what joy for those whose record the LORD has cleared of guilt, whose lives are lived in complete honesty!"* (Psalm 32:1–2 NLT).

There was a time when I wouldn't admit what a sinner I was, but my dishonesty made me miserable and filled my days with frustration. *"For day and night Your hand was heavy upon me; My vitality was turned into the drought of summer. Selah I acknowledged my sin to You, And my iniquity I have not hidden. I said, 'I will confess my transgressions to the LORD,' And You forgave the iniquity of my sin"* (Psalm 32:4–5 NKJV).

"Finally, I confessed all my sins to you and stopped trying to hide my guilt...And you forgave me! All my guilt is gone" (Psalm 32:5 NLT). That's exactly how I felt after I confessed and repented to God. I felt like a new person, like the weight of the world had been lifted off me.

Not long after, one of my clients, whom I hadn't seen for a couple of years, was in town and wanted me to look at a house she owned. I noticed she kept staring at me. "Bruce, there is something different about you," she said.

"What do you mean?" I replied.

"It's like you got rid of a lot of stuff or something." That is a perfect description of how I felt. Before turning away from sin and turning to God, I was full of stuff, full of self-indulgence and self-centredness and full of unconfessed sins.

I started to get excited about going to church. I began to be joyful and loud, and I knew it made a few people uncomfortable.

One morning in the service the minister asked all the children to come up front, and I went too. There I was, this big giant sitting in the middle of all these children, embarrassing my wife and her friend.

Eugene later invited me to a Pentecostal church called Revival Time Tabernacle. I remember walking in to this sea of black people dressed in suits, fancy outfits and hats, and they were all loud like me. I knew right then I had found my church. There was passionate and loud preaching from senior pastor Audley James, a Jamaican. Then of course there was the music, which was full of rhythm and rich with expression. It took me back to my Baptist upbringing and Sunday sermons at our all-black church in Texas.

I began to attend Revival Time Tabernacle on a regular basis with Shirley and the kids. Before long, I was there for the morning and the night services as well as attending Bible study on Wednesday and prayer meetings on Saturday morning.

I knew I was hooked and decided I needed to make a deeper commitment. I needed to get baptized. I had been baptized as a child, but this was again tradition, not a real commitment that starts with inviting Christ into your heart.

Like many Baptists, we grew up hearing people preaching messages like John the Baptist, and like most mothers, Mamma didn't want any of her kids going to hell. Even though I was baptized, dunked like a doughnut when I was about eight, there was no change of heart because there was no real faith or repentance.

Without receiving Christ as Saviour through faith, confession and repentance "you go into the baptismal pool a dry sinner and come out a wet sinner," which John the Baptist confirmed in one of his sermons in the book of Luke, chapter 3.

Here is a sample of John's preaching to the crowds that came for baptism: "*You brood of snakes! [You are trying to escape hell without truly turning to God! That is why you want to be baptized!] Prove by the way you live that you have repented of your sins and turned to God*" (Matthew 3:7–8 NLT).

The truth is, there was no change in me after I was baptized. There was no change in me after I began reading New Age books and spending hours meditating. There was no real change in me after I spoke to thousands of kids in an effort to give something back. On the outside I appeared to be changing, but on the inside I was still angry and carrying around unresolved issues, pain, shame, blame and unforgiveness.

There would have been no real change in me even if I had been baptized repeatedly. No, the change came when I confessed my sins to God, repented and received Christ in my heart as my personal Saviour. Then there was real change in me, and as a result there was real change all around me. True repentance is permanent, and you don't turn back to the things you leave behind.

The English word for *repentance* is derived from the Greek word *metanoya*, which means to turn and change. As such, it is a two-step process; the first is to turn around.

Imagine you're driving on the interstate from Chicago to New York.

REPENTANCE, MAKING A U-TURN

However, you discover you're heading west, not east, and if you keep going you'll end up in California, not New York. The first thing you have to do is take the next exit and turn around.

Secondly, now that you're on the right path, you need to stay faithfully on it. The worldly path looks like the Los Angeles freeway system with limitless lanes, exits, overpasses and intersecting alternative freeways. However, the new path with God is based on the straight and narrow, without the unlimited options and choices: *"Enter through the narrow gate. For wide is the gate and broad is the road that leads to destruction, and many enter through it. But small is the gate and narrow the road that leads to life, and only a few find it"* (Matthew 7:13–14 NIV).

On New Year's Eve 1994, I was baptized at the midnight service at Revival Time by Pastor James, and the deal was sealed. In John's message in Luke 3 he also says, *"Don't just say to each other, 'We're safe, for we are descendants of Abraham.' That means nothing, for I tell you, God can create children of Abraham from these very stones"* (Luke 3:8 NLT). The axe of His judgment is poised over you, ready to sever your roots and cut you down.

Yes, every tree that does not produce good fruit will be chopped down and thrown into the fire. I really sensed this was going to happen to me, that I was going to be cut down in the prime of my life just like Paul Bunyan had cut down one of those giant trees. The first fruit God wanted was sincere repentance, not just "I am sorry." I had been sorry hundreds of times before. Sorry I got caught, sorry for what I could hang on to, but this was godly sorrow, which led to repentance. Real repentance means change of mind, change of heart and change of behaviour toward God, people and sin.

As I really began to look at the fruit in my life, I realized it was all bad. Bad relationships, rage, abusive behaviour, unfaithfulness and rebellion against authority—these were the results from the seeds of my fatherlessness, which had produced the same kind of fruit in my siblings and in many of my friends.

The fruit was bad because the root was bad, and until God changed the root and I received Christ in my heart, it was impossible to bear good fruit.

I think the one thing I longed for when I began my journey of faith was peace. For the first time in my life in 1993, I was able to articulate to myself what was missing in my life.

Even though outwardly I appeared to have it together, I was still like that little boy growing up in Texas who was fearful and anxious and didn't want anyone to know. Well, two people knew, God and myself. So I was only fooling myself, and it was time to stop pretending.

OUR FATHER: THE PRODIGAL SON RETURNS

The only proof of true repentance
Is change
Your behaviour is different
And not the same.

TWENTY-SEVEN

A NEW WAY OF THINKING

I beseech you therefore, brethren, by the mercies of God, that you present your bodies a living sacrifice, holy, acceptable to God, which is your reasonable service. And do not be conformed to this world, but be transformed by the renewing of your mind, that you may prove what is that good and acceptable and perfect will of God
(Romans 12:1–2 NKJV).

Becoming a Christian didn't mean everything was all of a sudden all right. The effects of the Texas tornado had levied a lot of collateral damage upon those closest to me, especially my wife and our children.

For years I had taken everything and everyone for granted, showing very little appreciation for people or things. In my mind, I could always afford new things, and I often even treated people like trinkets that could easily be replaced.

However, with my new beginning came a sense of gratitude and appreciation that I had not known before, and I began to see my new life, wife and family as gifts from God.

THE POWER OF FORGIVENESS

After my U-turn, I was different. I felt different; I felt hopeful. I began to have a new outlook on life. However, this was only the beginning of my transformation. While there was proof I had a new heart, I still held on to many of my old ways.

I was expected to now do things God's way. I learned quickly it meant a whole new way of thinking. For example, it meant forgiving the people who had hurt or disappointed me, and I had a list of people as long as a football field.

Before my U-turn, I never considered forgiving people. However, when I considered all the wrong things I had done against God and the bad things I had done to people, it only made sense. By the mercy of God, through repentance and faith I had received forgiveness. It's one thing to think that way but an entirely different thing to actually follow through. It wasn't long after this revelation when I was faced with having to test my new-found faith.

I would come face to face with my first opportunity not long after making the decision to forgive others. I had gone back to Colorado to visit Glen, Larry, Lee and other friends. It had been over ten years since I had been back to Boulder. I arrived in September during football season. They were honouring the alumni from my graduating year. This meant I would be seeing teammates I hadn't seen for over twenty years. They introduced us at halftime, and we were invited to a dinner later that night.

It felt good being back after so many years, especially since I had gone on to play professional football and had done so well in business, which was a total surprise to many, especially the coaches. I was actually the talk of my teammates. Maybe it was because I had been away the longest.

I was surprised how often my name came up when old teammates came up to speak about our time there in school. They all had their version of me back then, right down to Cliff Branch, who had been an All-Pro receiver with the Oakland Raiders.

All said almost the same thing, "RB was the most feared and respected of all our teammates," and how they were all in awe of my ability and me. I was surprised how happy they were to see me and even more surprised how happy they were I had succeeded.

I remember that time like it was yesterday. Cliff Branch came out from behind and said, "RB, guess who just came in?" Eddie Crowder, nicknamed the "Bald Eagle," my old head coach, came walking in. This was like a scene from a movie. It was the first time I had seen him in over twenty years.

The MC then asked me to say a few words. As I spoke I looked around the room, and I quickly spotted him.

Gone was the confidence of the glory years of being a big-time coach in a popular school. He had the look of a man who had fallen on hard times. In fact, he had gone from being a powerful figure in the world of U.S. college football to being an Amway salesman or something of the sort.

It occurred to me how life changes. I was no longer "the bad Negro" he had chastised as a young man for a rebellious and defiant attitude, and he was no longer in authority over me.

A NEW WAY OF THINKING

This was my chance to gloat, to poke fun at him like some of the other guys were doing. However, what came out of my mouth was something totally unexpected. I talked a bit about my time there and a bit about my life after leaving university. Then I turned my attention to Coach Crowder and said, "Coach, I want to thank you for teaching me how to overcome adversity. I could have easily given up, but you helped me grow up, and I thank you for it."

I took the high road and forgave him. I had matured, and now as a Christian I knew it was wrong to judge others, particularly when I had been forgiven for so much, much of which is captured in these pages.

After that, I began to systematically forgive any and everyone who had ever hurt or disappointed me, including my real father and my stepfather, and finally the one who had disappointed and hurt me the most—myself.

Not only had God forgiven my many debts against Him and others, He also gave me the strength to forgive others, including myself, and that led to more and more freedom. Forgiveness is the key that will set you free from your emotional and spiritual prison, and it starts with receiving forgiveness from God and then receiving strength from Him to forgive others.

The first step to real freedom is forgiveness, because by forgiving others you are actually setting yourself free.

What you bind on earth
Is bound in heaven
And unforgiveness
Binds you to the offender
24/7.

TWENTY-EIGHT

HAVE FAITH IN GOD

Trust in the LORD with all your heart, And lean not on your own understanding; In all your ways acknowledge Him, And He shall direct your paths (Proverbs 3:5-6 NKJV).

I made a decision to trust in God to save me by giving my heart to Jesus, and now He was asking me to trust Him with my life, my family and my future. This was asking a lot, because at this point in my relationship with God I was still cautious.

I had serious trust issues, and that extended to God the Father. *Father* was not a word that gave me comfort, because my real father had abandoned me and my stepfather had abused me. I also thought, if there was a God, why would He allow me and so many other kids to be abandoned and abused?

While I knew I had a father and even knew where he lived, there was no reason for me to trust him. Not only had he abandoned us; there was no emotional or financial support the whole time I was growing up. Imagine living your entire life never knowing how your real father felt about you, never hearing him say, "Son, I love you." While I did see him on several occasions before he died, his absence and failure to support us as kids spoke volumes.

It's not realistic to trust someone who is never around and who takes no interest in your life. The word *faithful* means to be loyal, constant and reliable. Neither my real father nor my stepfather was faithful to Mamma or to us. My real father was never there, and my stepfather never really knew how to show us he cared. The bottom line is, before we can trust others, including God, they must prove they are faithful.

Very early in my relationship with God He began to prove to me He was faithful and could be trusted. He answered many of my prayers. A new

Christian is a lot like a new baby because when a baby cries he or she is usually hungry or needs a diaper changed or both. The point is, when a baby cries out for his or her parents, any good parent will respond.

I soon discovered that is what God is like. He's like any good parent, and He knows that, like a baby, we need reassurance that our parent is there for us. We are self-centred, and most of our prayers are selfish. That's another way a new Christian is like a baby, and God understands that too. Imagine being a brand new Christian and praying for someone with inoperable cancer and a collapsed lung and seeing God answer the prayer.

THE POWER OF HEALING

"Call to Me, and I will answer you, and show you great and mighty things, which you do not know" (Jeremiah 33:3 NKJV). I sold many houses under a "power of sale," but I never imagined I would experience the power of God to actually heal someone. It's one thing to read about these things in the Bible, but something you never forget is experiencing this as a new Christian.

In 1995 God began to speak to me. I was still in real estate and listed a house in the area where I once had been the top agent. Not long after the listing was published on the multiple listing service an agent came to the open house to inspect it for a potential client.

This agent was not familiar to me because she was from out of the area. She quickly made an appointment to show it to her clients. They made an offer, and after going back and forth we finally made the deal, conditional on a home inspection.

The owner was a senior citizen, so her children asked if I could be present at the home inspection. The agent for the buyer was also there, and we began to talk. She told me that when the listing for the house first came out and she saw who had the listing, I was the last person she wanted to deal with. It seemed my reputation had preceded me, and it wasn't good.

Not only that, she also told me she had seen me at several open houses but I never even bothered to acknowledge her. She said, "You walked past me like I was nothing. You were the most conceited and arrogant agent I had ever seen. You thought you were really something with your big Mercedes and full-length racoon coat."

I quickly corrected her. "Racoon! That was an otter coat!" which was way more expensive. I was newly saved, so I was still self-centred and cocky.

We ended up becoming good friends, and she later shared with me that she was pregnant with her first child and that she was a little concerned about the health of the baby because she was over forty. I asked if I could pray for her. It would be close to a year before I saw or heard from her again, but during that time she had a healthy baby boy.

One day I received a hysterical phone call from her concerning her son, who had been diagnosed with inoperable cancer. This was her first and only child. She was devastated. I offered to come to the hospital and pray for the baby.

After the prayer, there was a positive change. They released the baby to go home with the understanding they would have to bring him back to have the cancer removed.

Several weeks passed before I heard from her again. It was another teary phone call. The baby's lung had collapsed, and they had no way of telling how long it would take him to recover.

This meant the operation to remove the cancer had to be delayed, and there was no way of knowing when they could proceed. I tried to calm her down, and we prayed together. The last thing she said before we hung up was that she had no faith.

I remember getting into my car, and instead of putting in a tape, which is what I normally did, I turned on the Christian radio station. The broadcast was ending, but the man spoke of the importance of having faith in God in all situations.

I blurted out, "I have faith in God." I went to a prayer meeting at church that night, and we prayed for the baby to be healed.

The next morning, sitting in my office, I said to God, "God, I am willing to pray for the baby if You would arrange for him to be moved from the ICU unit." I wasn't a member of the family or even a pastor, just barely a year-old Christian.

To my surprise, the woman called me and asked if I would come to the hospital and pray for the baby. She had gotten approval from the doctor for me to come into the ICU unit.

My first thought was panic and self-doubt. I heard this voice saying, "Do you doubt I can heal this baby?" I said no. The voice spoke to me again. "Then who are you doubting?" My response was "myself." Then the voice said, "That's good, because you can't heal anyone."

I armed myself with my usual praise music, my Bible and some oil to anoint the baby and headed to the hospital. I was nervous, but I tried to act composed. After scrubbing up, I went into the ICU unit.

I decided to put my earphones on to praise God quietly, but it was like I heard this voice say, "That's not the way you do it at home." So I took off the headphones and began to sing to God in a normal tone. For me, a normal tone is loud. Shortly after, I kneeled down at the side of the bed and began to pray for the baby.

I got up and put some oil on my hands and laid them on the baby's chest while I read from the Bible. I turned to the mother and father and said, "I have done all I can."

As I turned and walked away, a deep chill came over me. I thought, *What if the baby dies and they blame me?*

The next morning before going to the office, I decided to get a haircut. While I waited, my secretary, Beverly, called the barbershop. My first thought was panic. When I got to the phone all I could hear was Beverly screaming. I said, "Calm down, girl. I can't understand a word you are saying." She told me she had just heard from the baby's mother that the lung was completely up, and they were asking me to join them at the hospital.

We had church in the ICU unit. Both she and the baby's father received Christ as their Saviour. The mother also confessed she had decided to commit suicide if the baby didn't survived. That was in 1995, and the baby is now a healthy and active twelve-year-old.

Faith is not something you can see or feel
It's knowing in your heart the thing you believe in is real
Some people have faith in things dead
But my faith is in something that comes alive when read.
The Word of God
Is Life and Spirit too
And this kind of Spirit and Life
Doesn't come from me
Or you.

TWENTY-NINE

TRIAL AND RESTORATION

The LORD takes pleasure in those who fear Him, in those who hope in His mercy (Psalm 147:11 NKJV).

I was in a period of transition. At one level I was growing in my understanding about my new relationship with God. At the same time my priority in spiritual matters had sent my worldly career into a tailspin. It seemed I was losing my ability to support and provide for my family. Our losses were mounting.

While I was still growing in the Garden of the Lord, on the surface I appeared cursed and not blessed.

Even though we lost practically everything, I continued to place my hope in God.

He continued to renew my hope in many ways. He helped me keep the three things I valued most, my love and faith in Him, my love for my wife and my love for my family.

I remembered the time my wife and I agreed that divorce was not an option. Even though our circumstances didn't change, right away I knew that once again God would honour our agreement and keep the marriage and family together no matter what.

It would be several more months before I saw the fruit of that decision, but "God's delays are not His denials."

The one thing I had resisted up to that point in our marriage was wearing a wedding band. I decided I would get one. However, something happened before I followed through. It was December, and Christmas was only a few weeks away.

As we did every year, on Christmas Eve we gathered around the Christmas tree to open our presents. I had long passed the time when I wanted anything for myself.

OUR FATHER: THE PRODIGAL SON RETURNS

After we watched the children open their gifts and I gave my wife hers, she came over with a little box. Naturally I was surprised; however, my surprise turned to shock and jubilation. You probably guessed it: in the box was a gold wedding band from her to me.

It was once again obvious that God had turned her heart back to me just as He had promised several years before when things for us looked hopeless. My wedding band is more than a ring; it's a constant reminder that God is with us in our marriage and He is the glue that keeps it together. It's also a reminder of His faithfulness to me and a reminder of my commitment to be faithful to my wife.

Although there was still tension at home around our financial situation, I continued to experience peace and the presence of God. There were still times when it seemed impossible my wife and I would stay married, but we had super-natural help. We were barely making it, and she was mad at me and rightfully so, because I had confessed some hurtful things from my past.

She was mad not only at me but also at God. However, from time to time I would reread the story from the book *Hippo in the Garden* by James Ryle, which helped me remain hopeful.

It was now the year 2000, and things would get even worse before they got better. I wasn't ready to leave real estate yet. The truth is, I was afraid. I had let my membership at the board expire because I couldn't afford the dues.

On top of that, it was time to renew my licence with the ministry, but to do so I needed a release from bankruptcy. Revenue Canada was the main cred-itor, and they wanted to recover some of their money, so they offered me a con-ditional release if I paid them a portion of my earnings for a three-year period. I had no alternative, so I agreed. However, that left even less money for us to live on.

By accepting their agreement, I was able to renew my licence. The children were no longer in private school, we had lost our house, and before long we wouldn't have a car to drive. I knew several people who would have helped us with a car, but I was determined that if God was calling me I would have to learn to trust Him to provide.

I had another test of faith just after making this decision. We were behind in our rent and had received a notice of termination on the door. Man, you could cut the tension with a knife. I had made up my mind: either God would bail us out or we were out.

This in the dead of winter, but for some strange reason I had peace things would work out.

TRIAL AND RESTORATION

We had a bad snowstorm, so I decided I would shovel my neighbour's driveway because her husband had left her. The whole time I was shovelling the driveway I kept talking to God about our situation. We needed $5,000 that day to avoid the eviction order. Once again, I waited. God answered in a totally unexpected way, and I received twice that amount that day.

My wife and I were not speaking at all. There was very little money, and all I wanted to do was seek God and not sell any real estate. I tried, but I had lost my passion to sell. I was only going through the motions. I kept asking God about what to do, whether I should stay in real estate or do something else. I was confused and afraid, so I stayed.

One day before going to the office, I really cried out to God and asked Him to speak to me about ministry.

That day I received a phone call from Pastor Ali. He had been trying for three weeks to reach me. He shared with me what the Lord had said to him about me being ordained, and he asked if I wanted to pursue it.

I spoke to Pastor James about it, and he said it sounded like the Lord, so I completed the necessary paperwork and waited.

In the meantime, I continued to sell real estate. By then I was working closely with the owner of an office who wanted to work in the area where I was well known. We had some success, but it was still a struggle.

While studying the Experiencing God course I came to the part called crisis of belief. The premise of this section is that if you think God is directing you to do something and you confirm that it is in fact God, you have to decide whether to obey or not.

I had been waiting on my ordination papers for evangelical ministry for several months. I remember there was a particular Sunday when I questioned God again about it. Pastor James had preached a powerful and moving sermon that Sunday about the power of one. I remember saying to God, "Could I be that one person that could make a difference?" If so, I needed a sign. Well, I got one that same day.

When I got home after church that Sunday, I noticed there was an envelope under the door of our apartment.

It was the ordination papers, and I knew I had heard from God. To my surprise, they were for my ordination as a pastor. I remember thinking, *This must be some kind of mistake.*

So the next day I went to see Pastor James and told him, "I think they made a mistake."

He smiled and said, "My son, God doesn't make mistakes. There must be a reason you were ordained as a pastor." And there was. *"To everything there is a season, A time for every purpose under heaven"* (Ecclesiastes 3:1 NKJV).

THIRTY

THE PRODIGAL SON RETURNS

"After he had spent everything, there was a severe famine in that whole country, and he began to be in need. So he went and hired himself out to a citizen of that country, who sent him to his fields to feed pigs. He longed to fill his stomach with the pods that the pigs were eating, but no one gave him anything. When he came to his senses, he said, 'How many of my father's hired men have food to spare, and here I am starving to death! I will set out and go back to my father and say to him: Father, I have sinned against heaven and against you. I am no longer worthy to be called your son; make me like one of your hired men.' So he got up and went to his father. But while he was still a long way off, his father saw him and was filled with compassion for him; he ran to his son, threw his arms around him and kissed him. The son said to him, 'Father, I have sinned against heaven and against you. I am no longer worthy to be called your son.' But the father said to his servants, 'Quick! Bring the best robe and put it on him. Put a ring on his finger and sandals on his feet. Bring the fattened calf and kill it. Let's have a feast and celebrate. For this son of mine was dead and is alive again; he was lost and is found.' So they began to celebrate"
(Luke 15:14–24 NIV).

Of all the great stories in the Bible, none capture the true illustration of God the Father as well as Jesus' parable of the prodigal son, where the rebellious son of a wealthy man cashes in his inheritance and sets off into the world in search of wine, women and song.

However, when a famine hits the land and the money has been squandered foolishly, he ends up in the pig feed, destitute and desperate.

He decides that, because he has messed up so badly, his father will never take him back as his son. He feels he is no longer worthy of the title, but even his father's servants get fed, clothed and housed, three things he couldn't do for himself in his current condition. He decides to go home and beg his father to accept him.

The amazing part of the story is that when he arrives home his father is out on the road, waiting for him to return. Not only does the father want the son back, but he welcomes him like royalty, and there is a great celebration.

In the Bible story, there are two reasons for the royal welcome. The father desperately wants his child back, and just as importantly, the son humbles himself before his father, admitting his mistakes. He tells his father he is willing to submit to whatever judgment he hands out. He knows his own father treats even the lowliest better than he is being treated now by the outside world.

The son "repents" for his actions. He doesn't return with a proud or defiant attitude. He accepts and admits his mistake.

The point of Jesus' parable is that humility and repentance are essential if we are to have meaningful relationships with people and with God. All of us have fallen short and need to come to God in humility, asking for His mercy and forgiveness.

I am partial to this tale because it mirrors my own story. When I left The Alley for Boulder, Colorado, my worldly inheritance was a piece of Mamma's fried chicken wrapped in tinfoil. But I turned my back on Mamma's teachings and what I learned in church on Sunday mornings for the ways of the world. I rebelled against authority and committed sins. My life was all about me. Many might say I was a success as a pro ball player and real estate star, but when I hit the wall in my forties I was lying on my backside in the pig slop, desperate for peace and a sense of purpose. Faith in myself had failed me, and I had failed my family. I needed a miracle. I needed God.

However, I had to be willing to repent, admit my sins and make a meaningful attempt to change and walk the straight and narrow.

The fear I had I know most people have, because we are all like the prodigal son, messed up, thinking God our Father doesn't want to hear from us, and if He does He will strike us with fire and lightning and condemn us to eternal damnation.

Logically, if this is the case, why would anyone go home again to face the music?

THE PRODIGAL SON RETURNS

There's something about God
We all need to learn
There's a celebration in heaven
When we return.

THIRTY-ONE

GOD THE FATHER

"And this is eternal life, that they may know You, the only true God, and Jesus Christ whom You have sent" (John 17:3 NKJV).

When I first heard the story of the prodigal son I immediately identified with the prodigal. I was lost, and I knew it. I didn't need a pastor to tell me that. I didn't need Mamma or my newly acquired friends telling me. And I certainly thought then that I didn't need God to tell me I was lost.

I wasn't interested in streets paved of gold or a mansion in glory. I had a different gold watch for every day of the week, and I was full of vainglory.

Before I came to my senses, humbled myself and repented, I had my own trinity: me, myself and I.

After I accepted Christ, I was more like the other son, self-righteous, full of spiritual pride, condemnation and judgments for the unsaved. However, after experiencing God as my Father I realized that Jesus was trying to give us a revelation of God the Father.

My idea of a father was based on my experiences with my earthly fathers, and this left me leery and suspicious about any father, including God the Father. All of my life I had yearned for love and acceptance from a father, and that yearning was still there when I turned forty. After years of trying many things to satisfy it, the longing was still there.

I figured if I couldn't earn the love and affection of my earthly fathers, who were nowhere near perfect, how could I possibly earn God's love and affection, because He is perfect.

I didn't know any father who would give his son his inheritance while he was still alive. Maybe a little taste or enough to try and bribe him to stay in school or at home. I didn't know of a father who after one of his children had a temper tantrum for no reason would go running after him.

I can imagine what my father, had he played the role, would have said if I asked for my inheritance. "Boy, haven't I put a roof over your head, clothes on your back and food in your belly?" as though this was my inheritance rather than his responsibility.

He would have run behind all right, probably to chase me into the next county.

This is what I and many people I have met think God is like. There were times in my life I felt that, like my real father, God had forsaken me and that, like my stepfather, He was the RoboCop, just waiting to bust me for the slightest wrong. Both ideas about God couldn't be farther from the truth.

Like the father in The Prodigal Son, God the Father will allow us to choose our own path because He has given us the gift of free will, and He will not interfere with our right to choose.

Like the father in that story, God the Father is eager to welcome us back through repentance and faith and will not withhold His forgiveness, love, compassion or His blessings when we truly repent and turn to Him in humility.

In the story of the prodigal son, the father rejoices with friends at the son's return. Likewise, God the Father is overcome with emotion and expresses it by rejoicing with the angels in heaven every time one repents and returns to Him.

Like the father of the prodigal son, God the Father is willing to receive us as sons, not servants, and He is willing to bless us with an inheritance.

Finally, like the father in the story of the prodigal son, God the Father has a first Son, and all that the Father has belongs to Him. Nevertheless, His Son was willing to lay aside everything to do the one thing only He could do, and that was to show us the way to God the Father.

In many ways, knowing God the Father is like having a real father because when we experience His presence we also experience comfort, confidence, security and great self-esteem. We never have to worry about Him abandoning us through divorce or death or leaving us for another family, because He is faithful and forever.

We also never worry that He will abuse us or beat us, because God is slow to anger and quick to forgive, and He doesn't carry grudges. He will never leave us or forsake us. Even when we die, He is there to take us to heaven to live with Him forever.

And finally, we don't have to wait until we get to heaven to experience God as our Father. Jesus has made a way for all of us to experience and enjoy

Him, all of the earthly benefits and some of the spiritual benefits, right here and now.

Knowing God as my Father has radically changed my life. He has taught me many things and has helped me in numerous ways. He has taught me about authority and responsibility. He has taught me how to give and receive love.

He has helped me to understand my role as a father and has taught me how to honour and respect my wife and appreciate and love my family.

He has also helped me to realize that I don't have to pretend to be perfect but to be honest about my shortcomings as a husband and especially as a father. This has helped me to stop blaming myself for my shortcomings but rather take responsibility for my mistakes and try to correct them with His help.

While I didn't have a good earthly role model as a father, blaming others is never the answer, but rather taking responsibility for our own failures and forgiving others for theirs.

The knowledge that God is the only perfect Father has really helped me to see the failures of my real father and my stepfather from a different perspective. With this change of perspective came a change of heart, and I was able to forgive my real father and my stepfather. I realize that even if they had been the greatest fathers on earth they could never be perfect father figures like God.

While a good earthly father should be valued and honoured, he should never be worshipped, and no matter how bad our earthly father, he should not be demonized.

Earthly fathers are human and therefore can never be perfect. There is no perfect father apart from God the Father, and there are no perfect sons apart from Jesus, God's perfect Son.

What I have learned is that this issue is at the same time complex and simple. What happened to me by turning to God is that I changed the trajectory of my life.

I was on the road to repeating the behaviours of my birth father and abandoning my responsibility as both a husband and a father. God made it clear that this was not His will, and while as I've pointed out I am so far from perfect it's not funny, the fact that our family is together was a major difference maker.

In this book I have focused primarily on the black family, obviously because that's my experience, but what's interesting is that the biggest predictor of social dysfunction is not race but the lack of a father in the home. In fact, a black child being raised by both parents, like my children were, has a better outcome than a white child from a broken home.

OUR FATHER: THE PRODIGAL SON RETURNS

As I write this in late 2012, my two children are grown now. Courtne, my oldest, is a young entrepreneur who has travelled the world working for a major music superstar and is involved in creating her own fashion business. Coby is at the University of Western Ontario and has grown into a fine and amazing young man. Both of them are gifts from God. Obviously this is a testament primarily to their mother, my beautiful wife, Shirley, but I also know that when I did the right thing, God honoured that and blessed our entire family.

> *You may be a prodigal son or daughter*
> *And have run away*
> *But God will hear you calling*
> *When to Him you pray.*

THIRTY-TWO

"FATHER TO THE FATHERLESS"

When my father and mother forsake me, Then the LORD will take care of me (Psalm 27:10 NKJV).

Imagine for a minute that you're a fatherless young person. One day you receive a phone call from someone who tells you that not only do you have a father, but also he is holding a huge inheritance for you, with greater riches and treasures than you could ever fathom.

This kind of rich inheritance can become your new reality, change your life and dramatically change your destiny. The secret is simple. God has promised to be your father and is prepared to give you the riches of the earth as His personally chosen son or daughter.

One of the most difficult jobs I have is convincing kids without fathers that God wants to be their Father and that they have an inheritance.

While producing a documentary on youth violence, producers asked me to meet with some of the kids featured in the program. One young man on the documentary team worked in a detention centre in Toronto where many of the high profile "shooters" involved in the gang violence that exploded during Toronto's now infamous "Summer of the Gun" are held.

They felt hopeless, he said, and couldn't see any way out of their situation. Some even said they wanted to go out "guns blazing!" like rapper Tupac. As twisted and crazy as this sounds, they said they felt that at least they would have accomplished something in their lives.

The producers first suggested we take the kids to our Sparrow Way project in a Toronto tenement area, but then I thought, *Kids need to know they have choices they can't see.* I knew once they realized that, they would begin to see life differently and behave differently and there would be the chance their lives would take on new meaning. As we talked about where we would film the session, I suggested we ask one of my dear friends and ministry supporters, Tom Caldwell, chairman of Caldwell Securities, a leader in the Canadian financial industry.

His office was on Canada's Wall Street. We wanted to use his boardroom for filming. There were five youth, ages 14 to 20, four black young men and one black teenaged girl, all without fathers. Tom said yes without hesitation.

Just before we began filming, I took them into his office, which has a beautiful view of the city and Lake Ontario. On Tom's wall is a black and white picture of the New York Stock Exchange taken in 1929 before the crash. I stood in front of these kids and told them Tom's remarkable story, how just 20 years ago the man whose office we were using was a drunk, dead-broke, with no apparent hope, standing across the street from the New York Stock Exchange.

I explained how, while standing there, he said to himself, "One day I will own a seat on that exchange."

I told them how Tom had engineered one of the great deals on Wall Street, where he, his firm and investors are now the second largest owners of seats on the New York Exchange.

I also explained that many of Tom's problems can be traced back to an abusive father, who died when Tom was about thirteen. It proves that fatherlessness is a problem no matter what colour you are.

After I shared with them the story of Tom's failure and success and that Tom considers himself a son of God and his success a part of his inheritance, one of the young men said, "Part of that sounds like the story of my life."

"Which part?" I asked.

He replied, "The part where life is hopeless and going nowhere."

I realized this was another example of the "six-inch cell." In his mind, there was no way out. What I was hearing was the kind of hopelessness that often leads poor black young men to the detention centre or, worse, into a six-foot-deep hole.

There is no denying that one of the greatest effects of fatherlessness on youth is feelings of hopelessness. *"Hope deferred makes the heart sick,"* as Solomon said in Proverbs 13:12.

That day, we demonstrated in a practical way to these lost, hurting, fatherless young people that they have God the Father and He has an inheritance for them as well, just as He did for Tom Caldwell. This is the challenge of my ministry, to connect people to the spiritual truths found in God's Word. *"All things work together for good to those who love God, to those who are the called according to His purpose"* (Romans 8:28 NKJV).

Fatherlessness is a global problem. I know the hurt, pain and antisocial behaviour that result from being abandoned by a father and abused by a stepfather. My siblings and I know this well. Three of us are now in our sixties, and our baby sister is now fifty. We all still carry the scars and bruises. Many of the risk factors associated with fatherlessness certainly were present in my life and in the life of my siblings, and some of these same risk factors have reappeared several generations later.

The genesis of this book was in 2005, when my friend Phil Kershaw (co-author) encouraged me to get involved addressing the gang violence that was plaguing the City of Toronto at that time. That summer 52 young men, the majority black, were killed by gunfire. It was coined "The Summer of the Gun" by the media. Although the numbers of murders would have been considered modest by American urban standards, it was shocking and alarming to Canadians, who pride themselves on having a peaceful society mostly devoid of the type of violent crime witnessed south of the border.

Phil felt at the time that given my background—first off, obviously, being black, having been raised on the southern U.S., and having made a minor impact here in Toronto, first as a pro athlete and now as a minister—I could help people to understand the root causes behind this tragic development.

I thought about it, and then it hit me the root cause and common link that ran throughout the whole "gang" culture was kids without a father. I didn't realize how widespread the impact of fatherlessness is until we began to work with youth at risk in Toronto. Most of the youth we work with live in subsidized housing, and 80 percent of them are fatherless. There are at least 13 more communities like the one we focus on, and the percentage that are fatherless is the same.

Since 1996, there has been a steady increase in the number of deaths involving black youth in Toronto. Many of these deaths involve guns, gangs and drugs, and over 80 percent of these young men, we discovered, grew up fatherless.

This was also confirmed recently in a story done by *The Fifth Estate*, Canada's version of NBC's *Dateline* and CBS's *Sixty Minutes*. Interestingly, Bob McKeown, the lead investigative reporter, is someone I played football against and, like me, was a member of the Canadian Football League.

He told millions of viewers the story of how a Spanish .45 calibre handgun got into the hands of a young black drug dealer, who had been executed gangland style. The gun he carried made its way into Canada illegally, having been transported here by another drug dealer from New York. This deadly weapon also took the life of a child. The gun owner had befriended another young black youth, a family friend, and asked him to hide the gun in his house.

He hid the gun in the bedroom he shared with his six-year-old baby brother. The child found the gun and while playing with it pulled the trigger. The bullet killed him almost instantly.

When I was approached to assist in helping finish this story, I became curious when I realized the victims were black. I asked if there were any fathers in the lives of these victims. Not surprisingly, the answer was no.

Interestingly, Bob also told me the majority of these illegal guns in Canada and the U.S. end up in the hands of gang members, who also happen to be black. However, what didn't come out in the CBC television story is that the majority of these black gang members are fatherless, a common phenomenon in the black community.

Many youth I counsel or visit in jails, black or white, either are fatherless or have an unhealthy relationship with their father. Most pregnancies, alcohol abuse and drug abuse among teens can be linked to fatherlessness. The statistics show that fatherlessness is probably the single largest factor contributing to everything from youth crime to teen suicide, homelessness, rape, teen pregnancy and on and on.

My co-author, Phil Kershaw, likes facts, and although the purpose of this book is to look at the fatherless issue from my personal perspective of how I experienced it, I would ask that you take a moment and look up this Internet link: http://thefatherlessgeneration.wordpress.com/statistics/. The facts are irrefutable: a lack of a father in the home and the accompanying disintegration of the family unit is devastating.

All studies like this will show that the number one indicator that a child is likely to become involved in crime, end up in prison or become pregnant as a teenager and all the contingent problems that flow from that is the absence of a father in the home.

Prior to working on this book, frankly, I didn't understand a lot of the strange and self-destructive behaviours that defined my existence until when, well into my forties, I gave my life to Jesus and experienced a total heart change. I now understand the forces behind my rebellion and bad behaviour, how I sabotaged myself as a young man and probably cost myself a career in the NFL, among other opportunities.

Frankly, I'm one of the lucky ones, because I didn't end up dead or, worse, in prison for murdering someone, like so many others.

While I and many other blacks became fatherless as a result of being abandoned and in some instances abused, many other people are fatherless because of neglect or rejection. Others become fatherless because of divorce or death.

Regardless of the circumstances, the effect is often unmet needs, unhealed pain and unresolved issues that make it almost impossible for numerous fatherless children to have healthy and functional relationships.

The unfortunate truth today is that even if a hundred thousand fathers were to return, millions of children would still be fatherless. But let's not forget: there is God the Father. Just like the Scripture says, He will take care of you. If your father abandoned you, God will be your Father. If your mother abandoned you, God will be your mother. If your father or mother rejects or neglects you, God the Father will accept you and care for you. If you have been abandoned through divorce or death, God the Father is always there, and He will never leave or forsake you.

I believe my siblings and I have greatly benefited from my mother's and grandmother's faith by receiving the mercy of God. Much of the success I have in dealing with youth at risk, and with adults of all races who have had a painful past, is a result of my own painful past as a fatherless and physically abused boy.

However, the only reason I can help so many people is because by the grace of God I have been spiritually and emotionally healed and restored as a son, man, husband and father, by God the Father.

The proof of this is evident today in my marriage, family, life and work. The reason there is now good fruit is because there is a new root. I am firmly planted in the Garden of God.

This reminds me of a famous song sung by the legendary B. B. King, "The Thrill is Gone." Well, I am no longer singing the blues; instead I'm rejoicing, and my song is "The pain is gone." God has filled the void nothing else could fill and healed the pain no one else could heal. Yes, the pain is gone, and so is the shame and the blame of being a fatherless black kid growing up within a society with many other obstacles that fatherless kids from other races don't have to face. It doesn't mean their pain is any less, but the truth is, they have less to overcome.

"The foolishness of God is wiser than man's wisdom" (1 Corinthians 1:25 NIV). My wife is a big believer in looking at history so we don't make the same mistakes. I agree with her but believe we should also look at history to see how we overcame our mistakes and obstacles in the past.

It was people of faith and all colours that bonded together through prayer and with courageous actions eventually brought an end to slavery in England, North America and the Caribbean. It wasn't faith in religion or the political system but faith in an all-loving, all-powerful God who heard the cries of our forefathers, like Josiah Henson and other former slaves, that eventually led to freedom via the Underground Railroad into Canada.

It was people like William Wilberforce from England and a tiny white lady named Harriet Beecher Stowe, who after reading the life story of former slave Josiah Henson was inspired by the spirit of God to write *Uncle Tom's Cabin*. This was the first book written from a Christian's perspective that exposed the horrors of slavery. Abraham Lincoln was reported to have said, "So this is the little lady who started this big war!" crediting Stowe's novel for starting the Civil War.

Before you dismiss the notion of faith in God to fight the plague of fatherlessness, consider this. What is the most successful program in the world dealing with people from all occupations battling alcohol and drug addiction? If you said the twelve-step program of Alcoholics Anonymous, you're right!

The more important question is, why does it work? First, it works because people battling addiction have to finally admit they have a problem that they are powerless to overcome and that neither they nor their family or friends can fix it. In the program, they then declare they need a power greater than themselves. While they don't specify which higher power, they recognize it's not human but spiritual power and wisdom.

This program was developed by Christians who believe in the same higher power that Josiah Henson, Harriet Beecher Stowe, Abraham Lincoln, William Wilberforce, Dr. Martin Luther King Jr. and many other notable men and women believed in. They knew He was and is the only One who has the power to break the back of the evil forces behind slavery, alcohol addiction and drug addiction.

He is God the Father, the God of Abraham, Isaac, and Jacob. He is the Father of all fathers and the Father of the fatherless.

There are many places besides North America where fatherlessness has become like an epidemic. While programs and education are important, they alone cannot break this cycle. The root of this problem is spiritual and therefore calls for a spiritual solution. That solution is a personal relationship with God the Father. He is the ultimate Father, the Father to the fatherless.

"FATHER TO THE FATHERLESS"

I had you in the palm of My Hand
Just waiting for you to come
I snatched you from the devil's hand
Because I have for you
A better purpose
A better plan.

THIRTY-THREE

HOW TO RECEIVE YOUR INHERITANCE

But when the right time came, God sent his Son, born of a woman,
subject to the law. God sent him to buy freedom for us who were
slaves to the law, so that he could adopt us as his very own children.
And because we are his children, God sent the Spirit of his Son into
our hearts, prompting us to call out, "Abba, Father." Now you are
no longer a slave but God's own child. And since you are his child,
God has made you his heir (Galatians 4:4–7 NLT).

While I was related to Uncle Leo by flesh and blood, I wasn't his heir. Therefore I wasn't entitled to an inheritance from him. However, what I didn't know until recently is that my first cousin Dardy was adopted by my Uncle Leo and Aunt Daisy. He was the son of one of Uncle Leo's brothers and a woman who remains unknown to me. So in reality, the only difference between Dardy Glenda and me was that he was adopted, becoming a legal heir, and I wasn't.

Unfortunately, Dardy never lived to receive his inheritance. Spoiled, he had cars, took trips, had horses and behaved like a wild cowboy. He told me he was even kicked out of school once for riding his horse into the cafeteria.

Dardy went to Langston University in Oklahoma but never graduated, instead ending up back in Dallas working in the family business. Like many rich kids, he got into a lot of trouble.

By then I was attending the University of Colorado. When my grandfather on my father's side died, I wasn't able to attend his funeral, but Mamma, Peggy, William and Dwight went, and so did Dardy.

The family was shocked when Dardy and William were caught smoking dope outside the reception. Moreover, Dardy and my baby brother, Dwight, were always hanging out together, doing crazy stuff to get money. Once

Dwight almost lost his life, breaking his neck when a caper Dardy organized got screwed up.

From time to time, I would get reports from my older brother William about him. Dardy even stole thousands of dollars from his parents' business, and people who knew about the black market said he dealt drugs.

Here's someone who seemed to have everything, but what he really needed, money couldn't buy. Like me, he lost his real father and was trying to fill the void and dull the pain.

Dardy was killed in a violent gun battle involving Dallas police. He was hit with several hundred rounds from police snipers, the grisly fruit of a promising life gone wrong.

I didn't attend the funeral and never talked to Uncle Leo and Aunt Daisy about it. While in many ways Dardy was privileged, he became one of the million black youth who fall victim to drugs and gun violence.

Dardy was one in a million in another way in that, like only a few, he was in line for an inheritance. He didn't have to hope for it. He only had to wait, unlike me and millions of other black kids whose only hope was to cash in on a career in sports or the entertainment business.

However, by coming to know God as our Father through a personal relationship with His unique Son Jesus Christ, we can become one of the millions who receive an incomparable inheritance, one that comes from the heavens. '*The blessing of the LORD makes one rich, And He adds no sorrow with it*' (Proverbs 10:22 NKJV).

Our inheritance from God is not cash or a trust fund, and unlike my cousin's, it doesn't end when our time on earth is over. This inheritance comes in the form of a blessing, and it can take many forms.

It can come in the form of a special ability or as influence and favour beyond your greatest dreams. With God, one day of influence or favour can mean more than the best education and years of hard work and labour.

"*I am the way, the truth, and the life. No one comes to the Father except through Me*" (John 14:6 NKJV). The way out of The Alley for me as a kid was through football. However, football was not the way out of the pain and oppression of growing up black and fatherless. After travelling thousands of miles from The Alley and finding a measure of fame and fortune, I came to a dead end. Just like at the end of The Alley just past our house, I came to a narrow trail.

The difference however is that this narrow trail led to a permanent way out of The Alley, out of the painful past of Jim Crow, death row and growing up

HOW TO RECEIVE YOUR INHERITANCE

fatherless. It was a way out of shame, blame and unforgiveness. *"And do not be conformed to this world, but be transformed by the renewing of your mind, that you may prove what is that good and acceptable and perfect will of God"* (Romans 12:2 NKJV).

CHANGE YOUR HEART, CHANGE YOUR OUTCOME

In the previous chapter I mentioned how when I accepted Christ it changed my destiny in that it gave me the conviction to stay with my family, and that changed everything. It speaks to the point that our actions have consequences, both good and bad, but the ancestor of every action is a thought. The book of Proverbs tells us, *"For as he thinks in his heart, so is he"* (Proverbs 23:7 NKJV), so what we think is powerful.

Therefore Phil Kershaw and I came up with a mathematical formula to categorize this, inspired by Paul's exhortation from the book of Romans.

CHANGE OF HEART + CHANGE OF MIND + CHANGE OF BEHAVIOUR = CHANGE OF OUTCOME

So what does this mean? It means that when you turn to a higher way of thinking you can transform your whole existence to something miraculous, because it starts a chain reaction that results in different outcomes. The key is to fuel that change with positive God-based thoughts, not worldly, carnal ones, and in so doing you can have the great destiny God has set out for you, no matter how dire your circumstances may appear to you today.

I don't believe that meaningful change is possible, though, without a heart change initially. Certainly we can compel people to do things whether they want to or not, but it is likely to be temporary, and at the first opportunity the person will revert to old behaviours.

However, when you have a heart change, you change your mind about how you see things, which makes you react and behave in a totally different way, and the result is a totally different outcome. You only need to read my story to see evidence of this, and now you can use this as an opportunity to change yours as well.

The simple fact is all of us want better outcomes, but the source of this is the change of heart. Einstein said "the definition of insanity is doing the same thing and expecting different results". Well unfortunately it seems the modern world is often based on "insanity", especially when it comes to the struggles of fatherless kids who are reverting to violence and rebellion as a means of dealing with the pain of not having an earthly father to guide them.

OUR FATHER: THE PRODIGAL SON RETURNS

Society naturally wants to change the anti-social behaviours and that is what the justice system is trying to deal with by punishment of bad behaviour through criminal prosecution and for many terms in prison. At the other end of the spectrum we try to give them social programs from government and other organizations as a means of compensation and encouragement.

Ultimately, if we want to deal with this problem in a meaningful way, we need to recognize that only a 'spiritual' heart change can achieve true, lasting and meaningful transformation."

A PRAYER TO HELP US ON OUR JOURNEY

"Heavenly Father, I would like to know You as my Father. Bruce says that You become my Father by me accepting Your Son Jesus Christ. Jesus, I believe in You. I believe You died on the cross to forgive me for all my sins. I confess I am a sinner, but the Bible says if I confess my sins and turn from my wicked ways, God will forgive me, and if I accept Jesus by asking Him to come into my heart, I will be saved. Jesus, I accept You as my Saviour. I also repent of all my sins and accept You as my Lord."

I will close by praying for you.

"Heavenly Father, You know the heart of the person who prayed this prayer. Will You now give the guarantee and the assurance that You are his or her Father and that he or she is now a child of God? Will You seal this prayer with the first gift, which is the Holy Spirit? Holy Spirit, will You now bear witness to this person that he or she is saved and part of God's family? Will You also confirm to him or her that God's continual presence is part of his or her inheritance?

Come on, My people, it's time to listen to Me
I AM the One True God who can set you free
There is some good advice human beings can give
But come through My Son Jesus and you will live.

HOW TO RECEIVE YOUR INHERITANCE

THE LORD'S PRAYER

"Our Father in heaven,
Hallowed be Your name.
Your kingdom come.
Your will be done
On earth as it is in heaven.
Give us this day our daily bread.
And forgive us our debts,
As we forgive our debtors.
And do not lead us into temptation,
But deliver us from the evil one.
For Yours is the kingdom and the power and the glory forever. Amen"
(Matthew 6:9–13 NKJV).

ABOUT THE AUTHORS

PASTOR BRUCE SMITH

Bruce Smith (1949-2013) was the Chaplain of Toronto's King Bay Chaplaincy. In addition, Bruce was the Chaplain at Upper Canada College's Chapel Services for Adults in Toronto.

A native of Gainesville, Texas, Bruce was a former team captain and all star with the Toronto Argonauts, of the Canadian Football League. He was also a member of the 1972 Grey Cup champion team the Hamilton Tiger Cats.

Upon retiring from football, Bruce enjoyed a highly successful career in real estate before entering the ministry.

Bruce worked with "at risk" youth in the Toronto area and had been a strong youth advocate, identifying the issue of "fatherlessness" as one that must be addressed because of the adverse and sometimes devastating effect it is having on the lives of young people.

Bruce leaves his wife Shirley Somers Smith of Toronto and two children Courtne and Coby.

ABOUT THE AUTHORS

PHIL KERSHAW

A veteran Canadian business consultant, Phil has been actively involved in business, government, politics and professional sports in his thirty-five-year career. Phil has served as the interim commissioner and chairman of the Canadian Football League as well as president of two member clubs.

Our Father is the second of his books published by Castle Quay; he also co-authored *The Kingdom Promise* with Gary Gradley in 2012.

The father of three grown children and the proud grandfather of five, Phil shares Pastor Smith's passion for working with youth and his view that the problem of fatherlessness is a growing phenomenon that needs addressing in North America and around the world.

CASTLE QUAY BOOKS

OTHER AWARD WINNING CASTLE QUAY TITLES INCLUDE:

Bent Hope (Tim Huff)

The Beautiful Disappointment (Colin McCartney)

The Cardboard Shack Beneath the Bridge (Tim Huff)

Certainty (Grant Richison) - **NEW!**

Dancing with Dynamite (Tim Huff) - **NEW! 2011 Book of the Year Award!**

Deciding to Know God in a Deeper Way (Sam Tita) - **NEW!**

The Defilers (Deborah Gyapong)

Father to the Fatherless (Paul Boge)

Find a Broken Wall (Brian Stiller) - **NEW!**

Hope for the Hopeless (Paul Boge) - **NEW!**

I Sat Where They Sat (Arnold Bowler)

Jesus and Caesar (Brian Stiller)

Keep On Standing (Darlene Polachic)

The Kingdom Promise (Gary Gradley & Phil Kershaw)

The Leadership Edge (Elaine Stewart-Rhude)

Leaving a Legacy (David C. Bentall) - **NEW!**

Making Your Dreams Your Destiny (Judy Rushfeldt)

Mentoring Wisdom (Dr. Carson Pue) - **NEW!**

Mere Christian (Michael Coren)

Mormon Crisis (James Beverley)

One Smooth Stone (Marcia Lee Laycock)

Predators Live Among Us: Protect Your Family from Child Sex Abuse
(Diane Roblin-Lee) - **NEW!**

Red Letter Revolution (Colin McCartney)

Reflections (Cal Bombay) - **NEW!**

Seven Angels for Seven Days (Angelina Fast-Vlaar)

Stop Preaching and Start Communicating (Tony Gentilucci) - **NEW!**

Through Fire & Sea (Marilyn Meyers)

To My Family (Diane Roblin-Lee)

Vision that Works (David Collins)

Walking Towards Hope (Paul Boge)

What Happens When I Die (Brian Stiller) - **NEW!**

The Way They Should Go (Kirsten Femson)

You Never Know What You Have Till You Give It Away (Brian Stiller)

For a full list of all Castle Quay and BayRidge book titles visit
www.castlequaybooks.com